A Starving
Artisit's
Survival
Guide

~ A. Wall

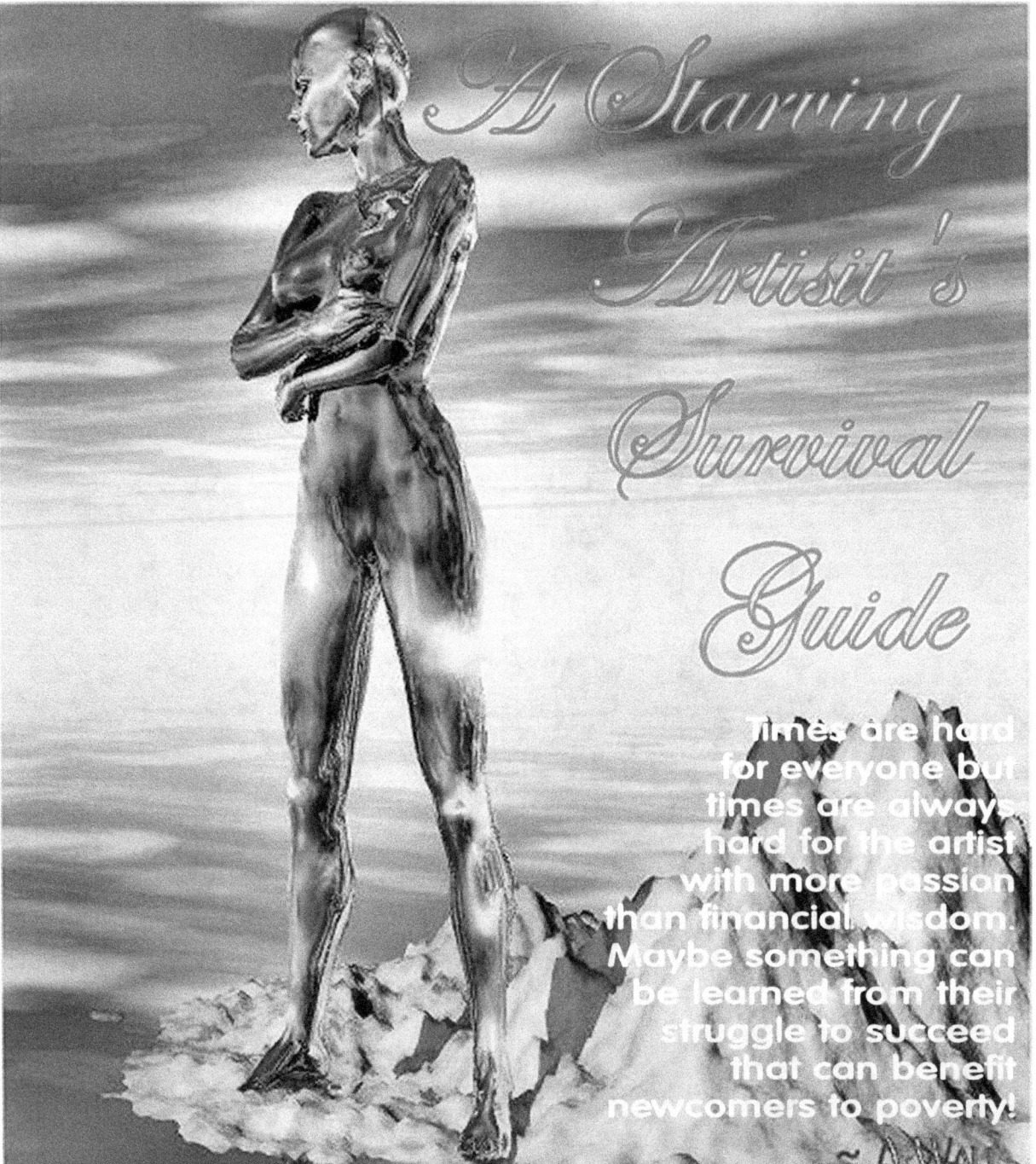

A Starving Artisit's Survival Guide

Times are hard for everyone but times are always hard for the artist with more passion than financial wisdom. Maybe something can be learned from their struggle to succeed that can benefit newcomers to poverty!

~ A. Wall

~ A Starving Artists Survival GUIDE for the 21st Century ~
or
Street Smarts for the Misunderstood Wise Ones Among Us...

~ DEDICATION ~

I would like to dedicate this book to the Philosophy of Dualism. My father called me an ungrateful wretch and a shameless hussy when I reached my teenage years. He was right but he was utterly wrong. When I was 14 at Thanksgiving Dinner my mother tried to explain as the topic for dinner conversation that fire may warm you but it also burns you...what is good is also bad, Angelina Jolie has tattooed across her shoulders "that what feeds me also destroys me". These are perspectives on the Philosophy of Dualism.

Madonna professes a belief in Quabalism that recognizes a Path of Severity and a Path of Compassion to reach Kether or Heaven but also there is the Path of Tipheret in the Quabalistic Tree of Life which is called the Emperor's Path or the Path of Beauty...I have walked the Emperor's Path my whole life.

There is great beauty in the withered woman's face dirty and out on the streets facing detrimental weather and a hard life. Mother Theresa was a beautiful woman all wrinkled and frail but these are not the accepted forms of beauty you see in the media where obesity and anorexia are both considered ugly. My mother once explained that there are two ways to say anything...you can say "when I see you time stands still" or you can say "your face could stop a clock". Being able to see more than one point of view is a function of Dualistic Philosophy.

Dualism is an ego-centric perspective in the philosophy of Autonomy where you may know what you would do and then see both the good and bad in what another says or does. That is the more honest perspective I believe...at least you recognize the third posture...your own! You are after all responsible for YOU!

There is a third posture always if you are true to yourself and forming opinions of others and not just trying to become a gang member where you have to go along with another's point of view to fit in, although in some places that may in itself be a survival skill, but more commonly it is the best skill of sheep (and really hungry people just before they get mad!). Broken people may appear to be sheep but it won't last. Have you ever noticed you don't see large crowds of homeless people when left to their own determination? There may be safety in numbers but more vulnerability when protecting supplies.

In our judicial system insanity is defined as not knowing right from wrong so opinions are very good things! Poverty is NOT the cure for apathy on a societal scale! The jails are full of angry young men. Disagreeing does not have to escalate to anger in civilized society yet I have historically been asked to cover at a Subway when I made sandwiches for a living because the staff there was too shaken by the gunman who shot out their window when he didn't get what he wanted on his sandwich. I know a true story of a man who stabbed his best friend for taking fish off his plate and a woman who hit a man in the head with a cast iron frying pan because he ate a meal she prepared for a child! People fight over food and the fundamentals of survival. Dualism is a necessary skill in hard times...and it is taught at street level alongside Autonomy. People are not treated as they think they should be...they are judged for being in need. I am hungry now and there won't be real groceries for 6 more days...to be able to eat a can of beans and call it food for a day isn't easy...to live within the rules harder still and to live by your own code of honor the only thing that will earn respect on the streets. Homeless people have opinions too and they know right from wrong...the most they can do is express their opinions but they don't because it might cost them kindness. Remarkably most think just like everybody you meet anywhere without great anger...but they won't bite the hand that might feed them. I have been more honest here I think...

The most you can ever offer is your own opinion, isn't it? This is why democracy makes sense.

In the Bible before the stoning of a woman Jesus told the stoners to consider themselves before they judged the woman THEY would choose to stone as they would be judged by God for their own actions...then he said he who is without sin cast that first stone. The woman walked away, thank God. This is group mentality compared to the Autonomy of the reasonable mind that acknowledges Dualism.

This book is written for both HAVES and HAVE NOTS who all have self images and opinions to express and personal choices to live with...it is not written for sheep, angry zealots, people looking for a cult or religion but for reasonable and thinking people. It is with this in mind I wrote this book and I have been honest.

There are many opinions to be formed here no doubt and not all will be in my favor but consider this...where strong statements were made...I knew this. I have no choice but to dedicate this book to the Philosophy of Dualism because rationalism is what will save me from my own honesty! This book has been written under the duress of the experiences noted and I didn't mince words. I have found talking to my children about my reality can upset them. I have seen responses where they don't want to talk to me because I might say something that upsets them. People don't like to see people they love hurt and go without...I knew this too. We as a family have churned through the fighting and anger and petulance of financial upheaval and come out the other side where obtuse conversation can be normal. If this book will make me money and make some of the bad things in my life go away...honesty was the only way to write it. I anticipate many responses to my writings...

This is a personal writing. Its intention is to teach people how to survive difficult times. Psychologically it is intended to also consider the emotions that come from difficult times so I didn't hide them and make it pretty. It is not written to shape your opinions of me. It is written because I have something to offer the nice guy in the cubicle who goes to work tomorrow only to find the doors locked on the day before rent and his car payment was due. THAT guy will be glad he read this book. I think my children won't like it at all. They like anyone else who finds fault here needs to look at the Philosophy of Dualism and see what they can learn then come back to this book or just shove it in a drawer and read it by street light if the need arises...it will still be useful!

If I were to have written that book...the one that pleased my kids and also talked about my honest feelings it would tell you how my daughter and son-in-law put me up in a really nice hotel with a Spa where I enjoyed the hot tub before my son's recent wedding and how many people told me I looked beautiful in the dress kindly purchased by my new daughter-in-law and how really wonderful even resembling the wedding of Prince William the event was not to mention how honored I was to get to attend and see how my handsome son had come to truly love a beautiful woman! AND I DANCED!!! That's the up side of my last month...not the topic or meat of my book. I am not apologizing...I understand Dualism.

What is said here is true in both capacities. Life and times flip and flop and the honest understanding is to know that and recognize such absurdity for what it is...a moment in time...even if some may haunt you more than others they do not define an individual still walking a road not knowing the turns ahead. A wise man once told me to always remember who you are and where you are before you act and I would add to recall who your audience is as well! My mother just told me to be sure I was right then go ahead so I wrote this book!

Narrow minded is the limited perspective that cannot see more than their own point of view at the given moment and how circumstances may change them. Narrow minded is being less than circumspect. Poverty breeds narrow mindedness! Brains that have trouble holding one thought due to lack of nourishment ARE physically narrowed in capacity to consider the world around them...like criminal thinking...it is extremely limited in scope of reason. It is accepted that poverty escalates crime partly because of the tearing down of self esteem. The intention of the Philosophy of Dualism is to make one think and it was my intention as well. *These things could happen to you*.

Here you will find a narrow minded fall back plan that I hope sticks in your subconscious in case you need it. It is absurd to walk the face of the earth thinking it could never be needed by you and here you will find help for such an occasion and nothing more. When is it right for people to be hungry? When is it right for people to not have water to wash their hands? When it happens to you it hurts...makes you want to cry...makes you mad at invisible people who should make it stop just like a baby cries when things go wrong and they don't know what else to do. The pitiful cry of a hungry child is how we teach and learn love and it is exactly what first occurs when your brain works less well than it should because you don't have water or food. I left most of the tears out but tried to be clear with words about the feelings one has when going through such hell. It is expressly hard to remember people love you but just sit there going on with life...even wanting you to share their successes and purchases and financial gains when you are looking towards a can of beans to make the pain in your belly quit. To get cleaned up for an expensive wedding and not feel that something somewhere is phony feels downright weird...I just did that and I promise you it was a joyous occasion for me and very real feelings of pride and so on. I only felt stupid for a day when I ate my Ramen Noodles made with bottled water when I got home to my waterless house but it had to be done and THAT is the Philosophy of Dualism...I am responsible for me...I am happy for my children in fact I am excessively proud of each of them! I can also feel sorry for me. Then I can write this book and try to fix it! Giving in to anger or self pity is defeat....I choose to keep trying. I salute the Philosophy of Dualism for teaching me I can and it isn't a roller coaster I am riding. By the way the bride and groom turned my water back on and long distance ordered me a pizza 2 weeks after the wedding because I waited that long to tell them what was going on with me so the wedding would be the joyous occasion it was. My kids all hate this! Fortunately I tried to raise them understanding Dualism...they manage. Second child of mine to marry this year and last year my son graduated college with 2 more to follow in years to come. I wouldn't mess that up for anything! I intend to be at their graduations too! Learn my tricks...read on!

Does a shameless hussy marry many times? Yes. Does an ungrateful wretch speak poorly of a gift given? Yes. Should such a thing be said to a chubby 14 year old girl who is newly fashion conscious and boy crazy? No...not in my opinion. Did I go a full month with no running water? Yes. Have my lights been cut off several times this year? Yes! Were survival efforts necessary as well as ugly and unpleasant? Indeed they were...but coming out the other end with a book written one step closer to stopping such events occurring again is quite beautiful. It is an achievement to SURVIVE! I stand accomplished!

There is no Path of Severity where you learn to love your oppressor grateful for the evils imposed on you that taught you so much while diminishing your self esteem (that's the

Stockholm effect) and there is no Path of Compassion where you learn to hate yourself for the pity you evoke feeling trapped by the eternal need to beg to live thus also diminishing your self esteem (that requires a Messiah Complex to go on)...there is only the Art of Living to the best of your ability for me (The Philosophy of Dualism and Autonomy).

I also don't bore you with all the body interruptions that occur with any concerted effort when your brain and hands don't want to work or your tummy turns or you get way too tired and have to stop. Please assume they occurred during the writing of this book because they have but they made no worthy point to note.

I say Heaven (Kether) is warm water when you wash your poor, arthritic hands that don't move well in the cold like mine or your young beautiful hands that can still do so many neat things (My hands still *look* young...I am vain too!). Say a prayer of gratitude that you have been so fortunate when you wash your hands says this shameless hussy who has loved way too much and still sees beauty in her own life! There are those with no water at all. I just was one for a month...how many more are there like me? Show your gratitude for every breath you are allowed to breathe! Remember old age and all the ugliness that comes with it is just the alternative to not breathing at all! You would be happy should you live so long I am SURE!

You only walk this way once and you will be known by what you say and do in life and you <u>will</u> be judged by all...even if it isn't their job. Opinions are good things! Strength of character is even better!

Smile at old people...they will know it is wishful thinking! Everybody wants to grow old. Don't smile at obviously poor people...it will probably just make them mad. Now if you see an obviously poor old person...don't just stand there fool! Do something! Didn't your Mama raise you right? (I have wanted to say that for a really, really, long time!) I have a brain teaser too. Why does the homeless person open their pack of cigarettes from the bottom? The answer is at the end of this book!

Don't approve or disapprove of me. Don't even *like* my book but have brains enough to know this book has value because things you find here have saved more lives than mine! Do love my art! (More can be found at www.Zazzle.com/Neophyle...poster sized and ready to hang also on coffee mugs and shirts too!) Buy my book for your friends! I really, really, really like warm water...this is me working for a living!

I am an artist...let me paint you a picture of life...

ALWAYS REMEMBER: There *is* Heaven in every breath you breathe! Where do you think Heaven IS?

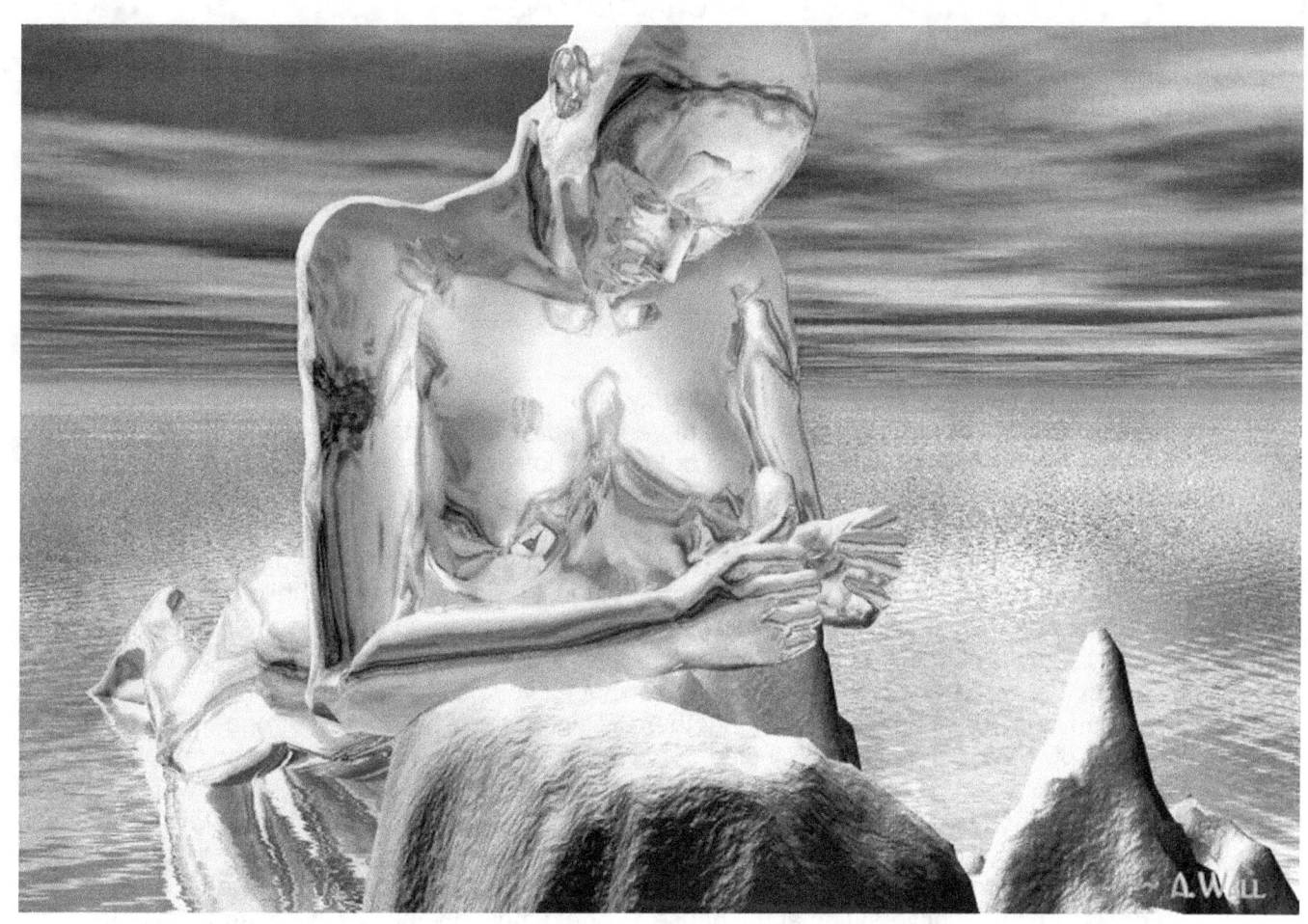

~ CHAPTER ONE ~

A Starving Artist is born that way. They find great passion and beauty in the world around them. Their behavior may be compared to that of an adolescent but I prefer to see it as a homecoming, the adolescent going through an artistic stage when they realize they were in fact a real person before their parents and the rest of the world had their say about it. (There actually is a religious sect called the Church of Ariel that tries to help adults find that 'real person' beyond the conditioning of life. I went to a meeting once and laughed all the way home!)

The Starving part comes later.

From birth all people have a unique and highly individualized perception of where they are and what they should be doing. The Artist is driven by some pretty standard needs. First, many would say is the need of self expression but I'm not so sure that's what really motivates most artists though there are some. I think finding out you can produce something others cannot and all that comes from that social recognition has to be taken into consideration. An art therapist would find content significant tags of personality and emotional state..an art critic would look to color usage and balance in layout..a parent would just brag at what their child could do. For these reasons early artists are intimidated into hiding their art and perhaps their self expression as well...if you are really good it, it causes quite a stir...or it may simply interfere with time usage by a guardian. The end result is the same...it shapes you...it changes the world in which you live...many just abandon the idea all together to fit in. Peer pressure is a strong motivator to the five year old. When one child is singled out in a group...kids have opinions. My grandmother was an Artist Librarian at the Elementary School I later attended and her theories were more Greek Philosophy than those I already mentioned...she saw art as a trust issue...will you show me what you really think? My mother painted portraits and stopped when she married my father who was a 'Commercial Artist' in my opinion because she thought herself the better artist. Art theory was dinner conversation at my house. For example my father did not approve of the performing arts yet he himself was a singer. He scribbled masterpieces on napkin corners then sweated bullets over a simple typesetting paste up. I do not know what the great motivators in these three artists were and I lived with them for many years. I liked my grandmother's art..she was moved by her subject...the effect the subject had on her as am I..she beautified our lives by tidbits she created...she saw you in your art work. My dad was more artisan and critic while my mother just looked and never said what she saw. Self expression? How could I possibly see that as chief motivator for all artists? My dad once drew a terrific Trout in pen and ink for a restaurant. Though he liked eating that particular type of fish you could not find his soul in that piece of art. There are many motivators for the artist. Starving is a very good one! A great deal of art even the classics were simply produced to keep from starving...

I call myself an Illustrator...I prefer to illustrate my own ideas...but I will illustrate yours for a fee...I can be bought. I think of that Trout my Daddy drew and the old adage: Give a man a fish and he won't hunger for a day but teach a man to fish and he won't hunger for a life time...does drawing one count? That one bought me lunch!

My choice of medium is a 3D computer environment using posturally posed expression modified computer generated manikins with a practicing Taoist perspective of elements for material uses because I believe it is/may be the 'idea' of an element that benefits health as well as the physical presence and both aesthic and feng shui layouts simultaneously...no small feat! Metals reflect but also refer to breathing for example and suggest then to smell...all parts of the brain that work in harmony when one is well...water reflects but suggests taste and fluid motion and so on. Feng Shui is very involved but it speaks both to the person seeing the piece - as Taoist exercises includes a true relationship to the environment - and the person in the piece which comes from where the pseudo(?) science evolved along with the study of Chinese astrology (their psychology with a huge body of statistical evidence embodied in a phrase and attributed to the stars) and landscapes even including the effects of weather especially the warmth of sunshine and wind. I see oriental sciences as an art form. Skies show literally specific time and place and then effect on a person and determines how they may respond from all of these effects while posing the art observer in a specific reference place including them physically in the piece of art. Nobody catches this aspect of my art! They look so simple! If you get it you should 'feel' the sun shining on you or the wind in your face and especially smell moist sea air from where I put you! Precariously balancing on a wet rock is a state of being...a certain tension yet people see 'person on rock looking out to sea'! Its tangible field theory physics if you look at it right. I'm not an expert I but could bore you for an hour on any piece I have made explaining what appears simple. My personal goal is to perfect my art. I can't afford a formal showing and I keep thinking that would make all the difference if the piece was big on a wall but the ideas keep coming so I keep producing...in that, it is self expression if studying ancient oriental sciences through art can be called self expression. (I personally think I am just looking for a conversation myself.) I have not found my market thus I am all over the place in various markets and styles of art since today selling what I can do is far more important than expressing myself like it or not. My husband got fired 19 months ago and unemployment is slowly running out with no job on the burner as of yet...

I'm writing this because I also write and have acquired an odd body of knowledge according to my daughter who is hoping to help me find 'my' market since patrons of the arts aren't what they used to be. Maybe selling a book is easier. I hope she is right.

Once upon a time I was a journeyman sign painter, I have had my own paint business in 2 different states painting everything from OSHA color coding and labeling, house painting, art on hard hats, bass boat engine covers and billboards...the largest I did was 17 feet by 40 foot billboard in North Carolina...I prefer the grid method of super graphic to the over head projector method...its more of an art that way instead of painting within the lines like a coloring book. Once upon a time I was the imprinting artist for 2 different specialty advertising companies again in 2 states where I not only did original art but then applied it to end products...I can create from scratch a template for engraving original designs by hand and I started with ears of corn to show you complexity (Corn has a lot of kernels! I <u>really</u> know!)...I know the difference between sublimation heat transfer and decal transfer and I have hand cut the Seminole Indian's feathers (again reference to complexity) onto a screen and hand produced a silk screened golf shirt for a sales sample...I have designed and sold and manufactured silk screened T-Shirts to the Boys' Clubs of America for the national bicentennial celebration to date that in 1976...I have engraved by Hermes machine everything from plastic to plexiglas to jewelry to plaques and trophies...I have heat stamped foil on leather and golf tee cards...I have hand painted ceramics as well as built them on a wheel. Once upon a time I made candles and macramé and carved wood and taught others how to do it again at a Boys' Club. Once upon a time I got turned down for a job because I was overqualified as a non-com sign maker at a naval air station (where I had also built air strips driving a vibratory compactor. I have done rubber cement paste ups with set type and used Zippotone for color separation in printing. I have designed web pages using original logos and my own photography writing in html as needed. This is commercial art...put in my years...paid my dues... I learned my first calligraphy font before I began the first grade.

Once upon a time I won a national poetry contest and was to receive an award in DC but I couldn't get there though my poem is published somewhere...never got a foot in the door in the writing world either but always hoped I would...I have books of unpublished works...

I am a marketable person...but I don't have a college degree.

The art of my life is an interesting piece but I won't bore you explaining this work except to say a few pertinent things. If you put my entire life on a pie chart you would find CHILDREN, MEN, and SELF DETERMINATION predominate with SELF DETERMINATION pretty much coming second with CHILDREN holding a considerable lead and MEN last but time consuming none the less. First and overshadowing all categories would be LEARNING as I have lived my life with my eyes open yet time-wise official LEARNING would be divided into PEOPLE who taught me useful things, READING where I never needed a class and teacher to do so, and SCHOOL which is really plural as I was never very successful at acquiring pieces of paper that say I know anything at all. These previous categories would be each greater than the normal SLEEPING and EATING ones with DRIVING outweighing both of those categories as time is fleeting. ART? Where is the ART in my life pie chart? Like the rays of the sun bursting forth through a cloud there is ART on this chart...oh yes! There is ART but not as a single chunk over time of so many years here or there. My children are sick of seeing my art...my husband hates living in it...my bosses always found it useful with even a few giving me the title Artist but all of them used my abilities...my grandchildren think it's fun and now...it is just what I do. I create ART. I invent...can't seem to stop! If I garden I find color pallets and Zen placements and Holistic scents...I dream gardens for a time then I draw ideas for them on my computer...every detail expressed and researched and true to a desired state of being with edible ornamentals being my current but waning passion. I'm a very busy person! My children marry...I design my dress! And so on...I can do this! Can't move as well as once I did...books sit on my shelves gathering dust and I research online knowing I'm settling for second best...can't afford to keep my car legal much to the joy of daughter-in-laws and son-in-laws who I can't bug more often than I currently do...but I can do this! So how to make THIS pay is the challenge I face. My daughter says from things she hears me tell her that I have survival skills others lack and could benefit from in this time of money madness and maybe she is right. Hey, my kids are all doing well...I can learn! I will publish the ART of SURVIVAL as I know it and maybe those still learning can find it worth a few pennies to throw my way. (For the record this is the same motivation that produced my favorite Sci-Fi writer Robert Heinlein...and turned Walt Disney into all that he became...the simple need to eat! NOT the persistent need for self expression...)

My husband just ran downstairs from his work on his computer job hunting to rub my back and pop it and check my coffee then he ran away before I could even hug him thank you! I have to mention that because I have the best husband in the world! The man knows whatever I am doing it is the best that I can do and never pushes me to be someone I am not. Aren't I lucky??? Love has led my life...survival is living longer to love more.

Now what could I possibly know about survival that isn't common knowledge? I could tell you I began my study of survival (massage and holistic medicine) in a more formal and determined way in the 70's while enjoying hippie camp outs at folk festivals as a flower child and meeting a Buddhist friend of my first husband who was an Herbatologist when a childhood friend of mine Al was listening to a crazy friend of his, Bruce, about moving to the forests of British Columbia and starting a commune. I was afraid he believed him and would actually go try to do that thing! British Columbia is frozen and we were in Florida! I learned 2 things from that very idea and the then recent prior birth of my first born...a son. I learned that I had been raised a very girlie girl and I didn't know how to build a house! The universe turned about then and to keep me from marrying my second husband, my mother sent me...get this...to Banff, Alberta to stay with the mother of my son's godmother who just happened to be a survivor of the invasion of Berlin smuggled out in a coal wagon! I was young and these events shaped my future. I came back from my trip a changed woman and took a job as a Carpenter's Helper. (While in Banff I went to see that very wilderness my friend was dreaming of only to realize I had to learn a lot if I would go with that friend there one day if only because I couldn't talk him out of it!) I spent time with a Ski Instructor there who lived off the land in a tent during his off season all the while raising his young daughter and discovered Acerola Berries and how to store them and stay well in the cold. Then I met a martial artist whose hobby was wilderness survival straight from the Ranger Handbook who would later become my fifth husband and lifelong friend. I worked hard to justify telling my friend Al he did not know what he was wanting in talking about moving to BC! I studied the Boy Scout's Handbook for my son's future questions too. I was working issuing WIC Coupons for the Florida State Board of Health Nutrition Division and taking martial arts classes 2 hours a night for a couple of years. There were survival hikes on weekends where I learned the Florida wilderness. I graduated in interest from wood to stone work and tile setting which really fascinated me because I had spent time doing pottery growing up then later I got laughed out of the Brick Mason's Union Hall by a friend of my mother's who used to be its President...it went like this...I asked to be an apprentice...he picked up the phone and called my mother and said do you know what your crazy daughter just asked me?...I asked him again once he'd put down the phone and made him actually tell me no...you could hear him down the hall as I left head held high muttering chauvinist! That made me mad. (I have since learned how to make bricks from mud and imagine one day building a house literally from scratch to put in the middle of the Bamboo Forest I want to plant but I'm so old now I would need helpers! And for the record...brick masons have muscles I could never dream of having...he had reason to laugh looking at me at 111 pounds in fine fighting form!) Then I bought the Foxfire Books on mountain survival, life style and traditions and picked up the hobby not of making crafts but in knowing 'how to' make them as my martial artist's mother taught me macramé, patch work, and embroidery (I had learned fish breeding and had the hobby of weaving and candle making while with my first husband who worked for a pet store for awhile...and a fire alarm sales job and as a rigger at the ship yards but no job for very long at all...but he made a really good chess player and pool shooter out of me!) and I became hooked on the 'how to' books she turned me on to for a really long time. I learned how to house paint married to my second husband even selling macramé hanging planters to our customers made with free plants I rooted and grew and making custom drapes, I even broached upholstery then did window displays for a store as a second job...I taught arts and crafts and almost opened Hart's and Flowers Boutique having rented and painted the store front even designing and printing my business cards but then we moved with my third husbands job to South Carolina and I explored cosmetic chemistry inventing a line of scented oils and a business called Kat's Eye Kreations (lost the Kat because she like my husband most!) and sign painted at the nuclear plant where he worked while making signs for restaurant and elsewhere as it turned out my second husband could sell me really well until he ran off and abandoned me with 2 kids for a better party elsewhere. I learned how to hunt and trap, cook over a fire and read and draw blue prints while married to my fourth husband a draftsman from Connecticut...I even almost got a degree in Computer Programming but got pulled out of classes just before the birth of my daughter by my doctor. Then later my ex fifth husband who taught me how to shoot also introduced me to his best friend who had actually been a Ranger Scout during Viet Nam and I learned a few tricks I didn't know especially about Bamboo! Nothing like playing with boys to learn survival skills! (Still not brave enough to try in ground pickling though...) So on my chart of what might I know that might be of interest, I could only say it this way...bits and pieces of my life that fall together in today's society as just some odd habits that serve me well when the lights go out or the water gets turned off...ya know? And I can make almost anything with nothing and make it pretty too!

My daughter thinks some of the things I know and do are useful to others so today I write but I will throw in some art which is my <u>choice</u> of marketable skill so you won't leave empty handed just in case you didn't learn anything you didn't know from all this writing...that seems fair...right? I did spend a year teaching arts and crafts at the Boy's Club so I hope to produce for you an interesting 'how to' concept book with credit given where it is due. I was born an Artist...Survival I had to learn...Starving is my current financial state and NOT a choice at all. Maybe this guide will change that...maybe you will like my art...

~ CHAPTER TWO ~

They say Necessity is the MOTHER of Invention...we are in a Renaissance!

First thing to go is attitude when times are hard. I always store a bottle of cheap Champagne in the back of my refrigerator. Why do I do this? It can sit there for years until...there always comes that day not when you have something to celebrate but when all is lost...expressly financially when you would never dare to waste pennies on such a frivolous thing...that's why it was there when my husband lost his job. Think about it. Over the years this helps shape your mentality especially if you like Champagne to not fear downfall. Poop happens...even the President only gets four guaranteed years of his good job! One should undo the childhood conditioning of being punished for doing something bad that inevitably haunts you the moment the rug is pulled out from under you. Oh yes! It's truly your fault that Washington made a law making it cheaper to move your tech support to India! Oh yes! You did it...you deliberately caused the Company owner to lose money so he had to downsize...or in my case I really wanted the guy to run a red light with almost no insurance and my husband stressed until his blood pressure went wonky planning all the while to herniate discs carrying water upstairs to flush a toilet because the water was off...planned every bit of it! My husband even planned the paper snafu at work that made it look like he laid out from work making sure the doctors office wouldn't fax his form to the right person...details are everything you know! Some of us are really talented at sinking our own boats while we are in them but real talent only does it when you had no paddle to begin with!

So if your life is perfectly fine and everything is going your way...put that bottle of Champagne in the fridge...it only last so long! The first thing you have to toast when you feel the need to open your Champagne is how long it has been there! The second thing is to remember how many times you had to replace it! OK so you drank the first bottle you put there because you had something to celebrate...say a promotion...and the second...maybe the new baby but you diligently replaced them always knowing one day you'd be drinking for a lesser occasion...it makes celebrating mean more actually besides the good advice and positive affirmations that run through your brain over and over every time you open your fridge! I call it reality therapy with optimistic conditioning as a side effect. It also makes you a terrific hostess when spontaneous events occur. Trust me when the bottom falls out and you don't know what you can or will do...that bottle is full of help. It's just plain hard to cry with bubbles up your nose and it gives you something immediate you can do about your issues. It also thins the blood...lowers cholesterol...calms the nerves and can lead to some maybe silly but creative thinking. I find it makes that feeling of a bucket of ice water that just got dumped over your head feeling go away for a few minutes and it can even help you get some sleep but that's me. Personally its the best use for Champagne I have ever found. My first advice is once you are past current disasters...buy Champagne for your fridge! There...now you have a positive goal too! Things have to get better so you can replace it...

I say that if our lives are defined by others based on the achievements and failures we endure...that bottle of Champagne keeps a running total and lets you know how you are doing! Can you see it when you open the fridge? Is that because you have no food...ah! Can you afford more food? Aren't these things to celebrate internally daily? We forget... If there is a bottle of Champagne in your fridge but you can't afford food...you know there are some calories in Champagne and being an alcohol it at least kills germs like mouth wash. A friend looking in your fridge will see success...do failures have Champagne on hand? They will also see someone expecting something to celebrate! Trust me if you look desperate and scared getting a job is virtually impossible and what friends? The old adage holds...smile and the world smiles with you...cry and you cry alone...isn't that the reason people are afraid of the homeless? The homeless are scared and desperate...wouldn't you be if you had no where to go?

Someone clever once said we are all one paycheck away from being homeless. I say put a bottle of Champagne in your fridge. Which do you think you will get the most mileage from towards reminding you to try a little harder to be on time for work tomorrow? Take milk in your morning coffee? There it sits making you choose which way you will drink it one day...

Personally when I see Champagne in my own fridge especially when cooking, I find I enjoy my meal a little more. They say the meal you enjoy most is the one eaten when you are truly hungry and I think this is true. We eat because of time of day...someone suggested it...something looked good or smelled good or even because we saw a good commercial. The one thing a destitute person knows that those who have never been that hungry don't...say no food for three days kind of hungry...they KNOW that a meal tastes really good when you are hungry. I once had a cold burger someone gave me and I asked for seconds...no condiments or lettuce or tomatoes just meat and bread and it was the best meal! I find Champagne a nice reminder that things have been worse and better...its still there! I am in the 'get where I can replace my Champagne' stage right now so I notice it *isn't* there every time I open the fridge. It makes me look silly and eccentric and I don't care...it has a higher purpose! I will replace it I hope! And there you go...when it's gone you hope...

You have to keep your head on straight when you find yourself financially more than embarrassed. This is my trick...

People are fooling themselves if they think disaster can't happen to them...natural disaster...financial disaster...crime. We walk around with a false sense of security that our cell phone will always work...our computer will always turn on...in reality that needs to be considered farther than even that statement. We take it for granted that when we have to go to the bathroom there will always be water and toilet paper but this isn't necessarily so. We assume that when we buy food we will be able to store it in a refrigerator and cook it on a stove. My father lived through the Great Depression and from years of hearing the tales of what he went through I came to understand that the most important thing lost during that depression was that sense of continuity. It is a helpless feeling whatever the disaster to find yourself not knowing what to do. I have found more comfort in knowing what I will do...just knowing...

Been doing the Champagne thing since 1981. Came up with the idea by accident actually. I was living on the ocean front in Florida and had been working writing and directing a community channel tv talent show when funding was suddenly gone so I quickly took a job driving a steam roller for a friend of the family. It was just me and my 2 little boys then and I had sold a house to establish us at this location because I wanted my children to be able to have memories of carefree days playing in the sand and waves and though grown today they do. Making it work was a big deal and I worked very hard for that. We cooked on the big grill on oceanside pretty much nightly because I wanted also to instill a freedom from the normal cooking ideas in their head...the rule at my house was if you couldn't also cook it on an open fire...don't get attached to the recipe. It was more of a joke and thought puzzle but it also aimed them at ideas for survival cooking which I thought useful. (Heck with my dad singing depression songs and Mrs. Mitchell my 7th grade teacher who first told me one day the sun would go Nova...I think I always thought towards survival issues...maybe my daughter was right!) We went into town some 25 miles away to spend the weekend with my parents only to come home to find our apartment ruined...a hot water pipe had burst in the ceiling steaming everything for several days before the landlord noticed and since we weren't there a great deal of damage was incurred. Literally I lost most everything there... there were no other available apartments...they said it was my fault for not reporting it and I said it was theirs...we settled on a draw...no damages paid and no blame coming my way. I might have fought it in court but the owners would have had better lawyers or so I told myself and then I made nice. I took the kids to my mom and went back to end my little dream...that hurt. About the time I looked in my fridge finding I had a bottle of Pink Champagne, a neighbor knocked on the door. I had to leave my friends too...people who live at the beach do not drive into town and when you live in town you are called a towny. We took the Champagne and toasted the good times out on the patio with the moon high and the oceans rolling...hadn't a clue what was going to happen next! But for a moment it was still all mine. I'm not that fond of Champagne actually and it was there to celebrate events that didn't happen with the tv show. (I have to note here that my camera man is currently a big wig at Gannett last I heard and things changed after I left the show where my canned shows took them to syndication and even a gig with Kool and the Gang in Montreal...I did good stuff but my kids had to eat! Sometimes its just all about timing.) So that is the memory attached to my bottle of Champagne. I moved to town got talked into a Specialty Advertizing imprinting job literally because of work I had done in North Carolina of a similar nature that I then kept for three years until I landed a really big account and the boss tried to steal it so I quit. There should be Champagne...it bought me a transition moment between worlds and THAT counts.

Last I looked my daughter has Champagne in her fridge...it's probably left over from her wedding...

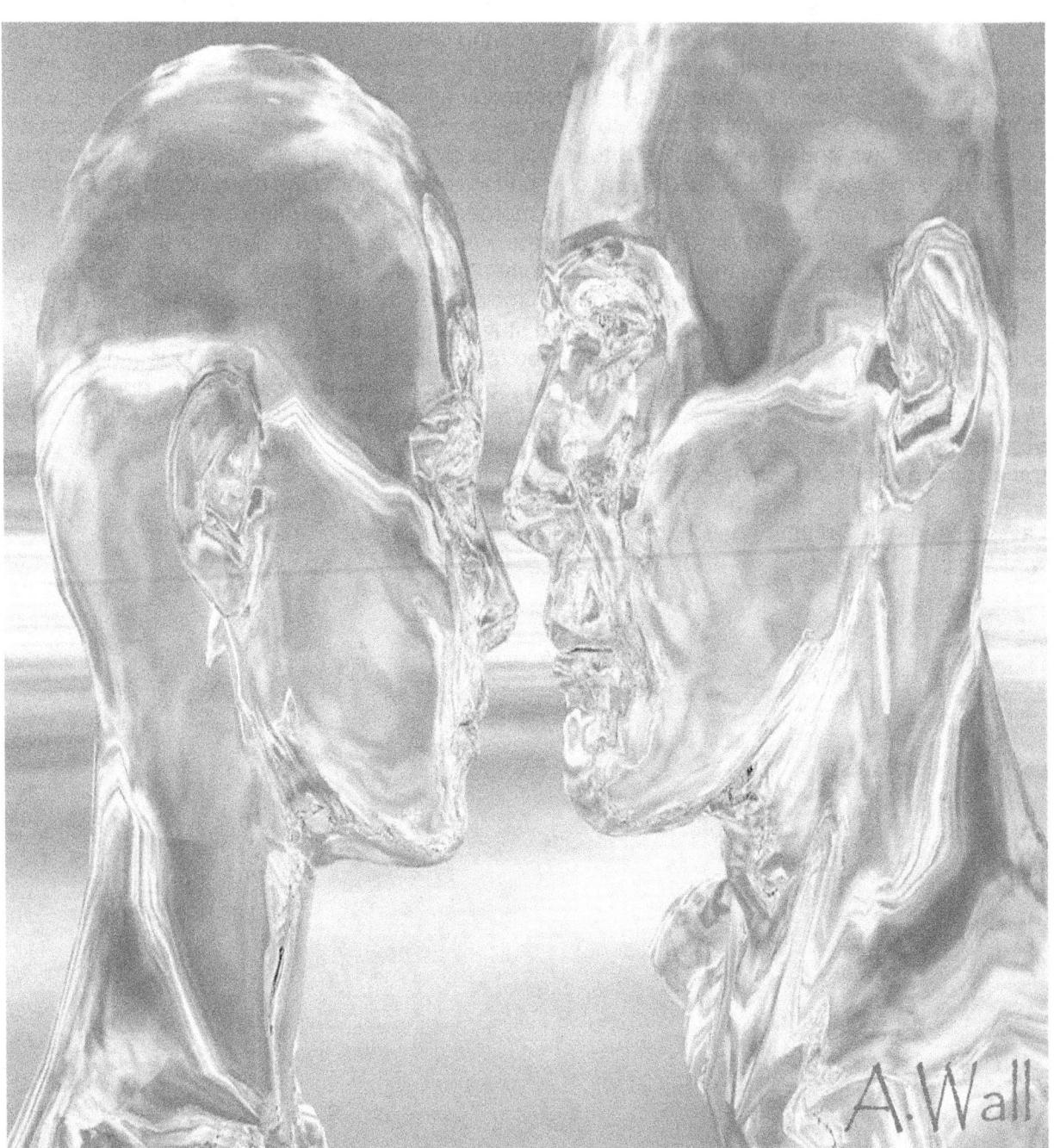

CHAPTER THREE

This book is the result of a phone conversation. My daughter was kind enough to call me. That may sound odd but after over a year of being a bottomless pit of need where every conversation is a matter of debating whether to tell your children what is really going on which constitutes persistent going without which hurts their feelings or not telling them only to have them show up and see for themselves how bad things are or...you can always sit back knowing that the phrase 'I did everything I could' is a joke because asking for help when you need it is just part of what you CAN do right? So a phone call can be a dilemma. Its rather agreed that they gave to listen and I have to tell them when things are bad but if it makes them cry they don't call as often so one tries to be pleasant and useful when given the opportunity to say you love them one more time which becomes rather precious during duress. There is nothing that a mother like me wants more than for her children to succeed...someone invented a personal living hell to put me and them in this position...that's how it feels. If I cry I'm the bad guy...someone will do something best they can which takes away from what they want to do with their lives or at worst if they cannot intervene...I've just thrown my child into my personal hell too. We keep trying, my daughter and me. I am unbelievably lucky to have had a girl like her...grown to a fine woman...married this year to a successful man and she loves me so she calls.

All that needed to be said to explain the mindset of the conversation. On one end of the phone there's the daughter wanting me well and happy...on the other end is the mother (me) no longer the woman who fixed everybody's problems that seemed to have all the answers but one in great need always it seems. High stress is putting it mildly. Thrill, delight, gratitude that my son made a phone available to me is what greets the ringing phone...I have a phone to answer...someone cares to call all things considered. Thrilled just to hear her voice...hoping she'll tell me about her day and that her brothers and their families are well because they don't call as often...you just say hey...It seems silly doesn't it as its just a phone call.

Having a phone is everything. You can't get a job without a phone today. You can't apply for a job without the internet either. A phone gives you the ability to apply for jobs and check emails to see your responses. When you can't go anywhere its also your main contact beyond the four walls where you reside. If you don't have a phone you are just dead in the water far out at sea or in jail. That's how the artist in me sees it. My son was able to add us to his plan at little cost. He is raising three children...that small expense was a big deal at his house. When you can't walk far enough to get to the library or the local job place...it is your news source too. It gives you the ability to pay a bill without a stamp or bus fare which can rock your world when timing is everything with utility companies and unemployment checks go to a debit card. I spend a great deal of time waiting to for utilities to get cut off...it happens...after awhile you just worry all the time about that and when they do a phone is your only hope of telling someone that may or may not be able to help you. You know when you become unemployed your credit gets ruined pretty quick so no one wants to wait for a payment but more expressly the contract phone companies have gone through a twist perhaps to encourage more contracts of giving you a new number if you let your phone bill lapse and then pay to turn it back on. Why is this important? If all your contacts have your number after filing a bunch of applications and all their numbers are on your phone, you have to call many people whose numbers you lost and tell them you have a new number...this makes you look unstable and undesirable for hire. My son solved that for us...my husband has hundreds of applications out hoping for a call.

Anyway, my daughter calls and tells me a little about her work...I thank her and tell her a little about needing toilet paper, sugar, coffee...the water bill past cutoff date and she tells me about my family. All the essentials are out of the way so I try to be useful and cheerful and so does she. We laugh over me needing tobacco for my pipe or the little dollar packs of cigars as we both see smoking as a bad habit but understand the cycle...stress and physical pain make you want to smoke if you smoke...and remarkably science has proved that nicotine and caffeine actually have positive effects on these states so its become a joke among us. She has had a cold...I just discovered that if you put instant coffee in orange juice it clears congestion so I tell her to try it meaning to be helpful. She saw a light turn on as I then remind her of Taoist breathing exercises she can do and a Shiatsu group of points to help clear the bowel which always help one fight a cold. It's the mother in me...what can I say...it doesn't take money to care. She knows my work ethic...I work 12 to 14 hours a day mostly making art applied to specialties at Zazzle where I don't get entangled with people that might side track my effort but sometimes writing...every day...like I said 'this I can do'! My husband stops himself at about 6 hours a day putting in apps, checking mail, staying current with news articles in his high tech field because he starts going in circles after that wanting to reapply or stressing why no one has called. The thought crossed her mind that my weird way of looking at problem solving might make interesting reading. I promised her 128 pages. I keep thrusting the burden of selling me on her shoulders because I cannot sell my soul...it doesn't work...I have tried. I have little respect for artistic criticism because if I listen to it...I will believe it. I can't compare my stuff to another artists and the commercial stuff is like being turned down for a part in a movie...your thighs are too thick or you just don't have the right look...if I believed that I would quit working. I think with my circumstances losing heart is the last thing I need so someone else has to sell me..I just keep producing but I told her a long time ago I would take advice from her as to what I should produce so...all she had to do was ask and I am writing.

I really don't know what you might need to know. Our food conversation also drifted to the other family joke...Mom can't afford patents. It has become apparent to my kids that I am in fact ahead of my time inventing things. I tell them my ideas and they call me when they pop up on tv...its a family game! Ok so some people play Scrabble and we kind of do that too. On Facebook there is a game called Words With Friends and my daughter got me to try it through our phone. I love that game! (Not just because it allows me to stretch my brain which it does when playing my four grown kids but it also lets me know they are alive and well without that phone call the boys don't have the heart to make often enough to suit their mother. See, I serve as a constant reminder to my whole dad gum family that they aren't quite successful enough but they are working on it every one of them. My boys especially would not allow me to go without if they could do something about it...I know this! So we play...every day I look for Words from each of them and they look for Words from me...just enough, you know?) The food conversation led to one such 'invention' of their mad artist mother that has now become part of the World Food Program...their new peanut butter packet idea! See before my daughter's wedding my oldest son thought he would be able to help me get a patent on a Fashion Concept I invented. I'm debating telling the tale or an abridged version...I'll write it long and we can shorten it later if need be. This is me explaining my point of view as I said I would. It is very much written as I say it.

In 2006 I invented a form of fashion that is still not on the market. I call it Ty-Wear but being still hopeful, I won't explain it in detail. The story goes my husband and I had researched the potential of being street artists with balloons available for people who make donations...whew...that is carefully worded because that may still be an option in our future and street vendor is a different thing than street performer according to local laws. So I invented 2 characters, squeezed costume pieces from my family a few months before my daughter's wedding and was ever so hopeful my son the welder would help me acquire a helium tank. In the process of building the characters costumes I acquired a cheap wig that wasn't the look I wanted. I modified it to work. (It is flatly a clever idea I also won't fully explain! I haven't found my door out of this financial mess yet! That may be it!) To encourage us old people trying to publically make fools of ourselves on street corners for money and to encourage my son to get us the tank because we are fool enough to make a living this way...I planned a family picnic! I squeezed food from our budget into new forms to go with the notions of futuristic mimes...our characters...and made plans for photos for labels for the inexpensively cottage industry manufactured hair products also a test of whether they were even workable. Only my daughter-in-law and grand children showed up for many reasons and at an hour so late the only hope was the meal and the photos...we did not burst onto the scene in costume. The food I prepared was hamburger and hot dog balls in one crazy plastic bowl and potato salad and devilled eggs in plastic Easter eggs in another and wasabi peas scattered as relish among the balls, Kool-Aid stars ice cubes in clear flavored water with bright colored shooters for glasses and jelly beans for desert to go with our look of futuristic mime. I made the photos, got releases signed, costumed people but mostly I got my daughter-in-law to use the hair ornaments herself...she could see dollar signs! The Ty-Ware worked for kids clothing for the photo shoot and I used melt in your mouth wrapped mints to build their outfits. (The labels were later made as well! Look GREAT!) Everyone loved the food but our real goal was not accomplished...we did not go public without mimes. My daughter-in-law told my son I was sitting on a gold mine! I loved that idea and he started talking patent fees. That shifted our direction entirely! Mimes went to the back burner...someone was going to back us...my son!

Now I have to explain my lovely daughter's wedding was a little like the movie Mama Mia for me...2 ex husbands...a current one...and others who loved my daughter over the years would be there. I needed a dress...had no money and a son offering to back the hair patent but not so much the fashion idea. I got my other son to buy me fabric and utilizing my Ty-Ware concept...I made my dress for the wedding custom bead work and all. KEPT ME BUSY! (The dress worked too and showed my son that the idea was also a good one!) So behind me as I type there are boxed Mime Costumes and Ty-Ware Outfits as well as the entire cottage industry for the Hair Ornaments with 50 manufactured items and unprinted labels on this computer to go with them...I left out the Mime-yesterday-tomorrow-local video game I wrote in flow chart form from days gone by when I studied Basic which now needs to be converted into Java and Flash (still learning those languages online but a mini webpage for the mobile is built already! I even designed a tv commercial with jingles to promote the products per my son, the investor's, decision that we will need one...programming is an art too I think if its done right...). Food is the topic I'm trying to get to...I invented a nutritional snack base product concept to be used with kids Ty-Ware that would teach by experience a twist in high fashion vs. hunger to make a kid think. If your cute apparel can also feed you but it loses some of it fashion appeal...if the most readily available snack was also good for you and parent approved...it shifts the fast food vendor concept to a which is more important and the answer is in my hands not mommy's pocket book idea. I like things that make children problem solvers instead of dependent. So...

If you take dried mashed potatoes, powdered honey and peanut butter and turn it into play dough of a sort...you can make a ball snack that is full of vitamin B (calming vitamin), instant energy, and longer burning carbs with a little protein and a slew of potato nutrition that includes potassium. Add the slightest bit of that hardener from beets...dry them out and a handful is the equivalent of a peanut butter sandwich...easily digestible with only peanut allergies as an issue. Not exactly a candy now is it? Might taste like one though...exceptionally filling if you are actually hungry too! Glad World Food agrees but I'm not sure of all their ingredients.

This is what a starving artist does to survive...they keep trying! Now I mentioned martial arts in my history and the reflection of Taoism in my art...it's my own variety of food function that my daughter gets a kick out of and thought publish worthy. I tend to work nights and sleep days mostly because days are scary...last registered letter was my storage unit. You downsize space to try to live within your means which we did but then you have valuable stuff you no longer have room for. We kept planning to try EBay but could never get to it much less physically move things to make that happen so it sat. Eventually just surviving with a roof and basics outweighs the ability to pay that bill so it's all gone now. I sleep days also because I don't have to talk to the man who insists on putting a notice on my door and knocking before he ruins my life cutting off water or lights...those guys LIKE to see you cry! I'm convinced of it! Either that or they just want to hear one more time that you are a helpless person and they have power over you...I don't know but it serves no purpose so I avoid it. I sleep days because it's easier to deal with weather and less disruptive when things are cut off to be awake at night. I sleep days so my husband doesn't have to face me for hours with no good news and nowhere else to be...besides...I've always been a night owl and I work well alone. I have produced literally hundreds of items on Zazzle all for sale right now! That's being out there with products for sale...

In the middle of the night all alone with a mostly empty pantry you get creative. You learn what your body craves from being actually hungry then you figure how to get those things into you. You learn what changes different foods cause almost immediately when you are running on empty. I was raised poor so all the how to make something from nothing recipes are already mine but this is one step further now. Then there are ethnic echoes in what I eat:

Japanese Sushi is a favorite because it costs so little to make if you use canned salmon or tuna or lunch meats...I was doing that before I saw on Diners and Dives what they have now named an 'Urban Roll' using regular cooked meats. I have cucumbers and sometimes green onions growing in my garden...rice and Nori are cheap...Wasabi stimulates digestion and a little goes a really long way...good soy sauce (no wheat!) is full of good stuff to include salts the body needs especially if you sweat with no A/C. Our dog loves Sushi Night! Nutritionally you are filling up on rice with some greens and a little protein...filling and balanced for a stressful life! My favorite memory is my granddaughter walking into a kitchen while I was rolling Sushi and says, 'grandmommy is cooking!', with much glee (she likes Sushi too...). Can you imagine? It used to be grandmothers baking a kid recalls but not my girl! Ham and Cheese Sushi is a good one...I tend to make Tempura with chicken though...can't quite do that flavor with seaweed. And I personally can only use Tilapia of the frozen fishes. Shrimp get boiled for a salad or nuked and thrown into Alfredo Sauce with Pasta...

Beans make an excellent source of protein but I have to watch how often I do beans as I am Arthritic...same with shell fish and liver. Liver is an excellent source of Iron and extremely cheap so it's an important item every now and then. Bean paste is most known in every culture but we call it dip here. Oriental foods use soy bean paste and curd called Tofu for protein...Mexico makes refried beans and Bean Burritos...in Afghanistan its chick peas and garlic called Hummus...again...for nutrition the wild west was won on cattle drives and a pot of beans for dinner...any bean will do. I like Kidney Beans and Hard Boiled Eggs with Onion and Mayonnaise as a salad. I like peas and onions with mayo also as a salad and peas are a different nutritional make up more heavily full of vitamin B so it's good for the nerves my mother used to say. I have a terrific recipe for Pork and Beans where you put your favorite Baked Bean condiments in a baking dish with canned beans then put Pork Chops on top covered in mustard, brown sugar, and slivered lime (skin and all) and onion slices...gets a little citrus in there too! Bake this covered and your family will beg for more! Beans are cheaper than meats and they work. Beans make you feel full longer than Sushi but it is hard to make pretty a bowl of beans...

I live by bouillon. Knorrs puts out terrific cubes that make you actually feel better when consumed so they must be made with enzymes intact. Cheap bouillon doesn't necessarily have what their cubes have besides the flavor is better and again good for salts the body needs. I use dollar store condiments because a good sauce makes a dish out of anything and you need condiments to do that but I splurge on my bouillon. Thickened bouillon is called gravy! In a fondue pot bouillon makes a meal from a dried piece of bread and there is nutrition there too...not to mention the social effect compared to a cup of bouillon and crust of bread...

Mustard has many uses and it all begins with mustard powder so cheap works. The ingredient that turns mustard yellow is good for the liver...that's in cheap mustard too...turmeric...read the label. According to Traditional Chinese Medicine the liver is the angry organ of the body when not functioning well. Ever see an angry drunk? Hmmm... (There's a Taoist exercise for the liver that actually visually changes the tongue diagnostic I'll explain later...) An over active liver assaults the pancreas...the first organ the body attacks under extreme starvation is the pancreas...its a balance. The balance can be altered by food or mood and mood can reflect food in my opinion from all I have read. Let the good times roll! Featured phrase of New Orleans where Cajun spicy and Muffalatta mustard sauce are common...I believe it! Digestion is of the utmost importance and ignored greatly in the US as shown by all the tummy products available! The Taoist approach is to balance the organs...I try to do that with food. Cascara Sagrada is the herb my mother taught me 'turned the liver over' which best I can tell means it aids the liver in producing the enzymes that make you go but it definitely can benefit the liver and the digestion. In antiquated religious tomes digestion is mentioned as a function of dilusion (however shallow breathing caused by poor digestion can alter your state of being but I'll discuss breathing later too). I consider it toxic waste and when you are busy poisoning yourself you can get pretty mad! Mustard helps the liver function and liver gets rid of the poisons...its important! Another odd effect of poor liver function is the starving distended belly...when you are really hungry your body produces gas...there's an odd cycle to this. To the left of your belly button there is a valve between your upper and lower intestines and the intestines act like one of those long balloons made of skin so if your stomach acids have nothing to consume you bloat...the bloating if left to continue for a longer than normal period bloat all the way to this valve and open it from the wrong side which is a really bad thing because in the lower intestines where the worst of the toxic waste resides all sorts of bacteria also live. You don't want bacteria from the lower intestines into the upper intestines and I have never read this written concerning starvation but it is known that bacterial infection is common during starvation. Lower intestinal bacteria create byproducts that also produce gases and this is how you see those awful pictures of children with huge distended bellies and hear about them eating pebbles and dirt...anything to break the cycle! Digestion is everything...2 hours after a meal you should evacuate it! It's that simple. If your waist muscles can't stay taught for some reason, a belt at your waist can help keep that valve closed I have found. There is also Taoist exercises and massage to aid this function. So I buy cheap Mustard and use it in odd places...goes great in Ramen Noodles!

Tomato Paste is an excellent source of vitamin C on a minimal budget. A teaspoon a day can do wonders for your complexion. When things get ridiculous Ketchup works as a substitute. Remarkably vitamin C makes your Kidneys work and you will learn that Ketchup has vitamin C because it can make you need to urinate. Sounds like a wives tale but it has worked that way for me. Tomatoes from your garden are also full of liquid when the water is off and a can of Tomatoes and a few spices, a Spaghetti Sauce make! Ramen Noodles with or without the spice pack depending on the flavor and your taste make an excellent Noodle for your sauce as well. For Ramen you really only need warm water to makes the noodles into a meal. Dump a can of Tomatoes into a bowl with Ramen and the Beef Bouillon package or substitute your own bouillon, or even use a glass jar and sit them in the sun in a window...instant spaghetti dinner of a sort! And a healthy meal too with carbs and Vitamin C and all precious water without even adding more...

Hot sauce in Ramen Noodles not only gives you energy but stimulates the digestion too. Most Dollar stores carry Tabasco Sauce...again a red pepper is a red pepper...read the label. Red pepper is different than black or white as it not only aids digestion but does it partly by calming the stomach. Those who really like hot stuff...Pepper Heads can tell you there is an emotional and physical response to red pepper. In the extreme it can cause a sense of euphoria I have heard related to the feeling after sex! They will also tell you the light headedness is accompanied by warmth to the touch in the abdomen which is what is required for increased circulation. I am not a Pepper Head...but the value of using red pepper instead of the traditional peppers I have found value in. Horse radish doesn't seem to calm the stomach but does heat it so it likely helps digestion too.

When it comes to Mayonnaise I look for two words...trans-fats and MSG. Trans-fats are useless and they take nutrients as they go through you because you cannot digest them and I have a problem with MSG as many others do. Mayonnaise is made from eggs, oil, mustard powder and vinegar. It is a food actually though eaten in small quantity but it has nutritional value...egg is protein! Vinegar neutralizes acids too...wonder what it does to belly acids?

I am a coffee addict. It was a discussion of coffee that brought me to this writing. I crave caffeine. I have exceptionally low blood pressure and have from childhood...caffeine is my cure. It sounds like a small thing but when you get down to having to make sure you don't get dehydrated, a cup of coffee becomes a serious consideration. Remarkably I have found that pushing coffee solves many ailments to include the physical demand of hunger...drink a cup and you are less hungry especially if you have the luxury of sugar and cream! Hungry people with houses drink coffee...hungry people on the streets tend more towards beer partly because both are expected and partly because both work only beer flushes kidneys better and has more calories besides like in Mexico when you can't guarantee your water source is a clean faucet beer is treated water and it has more calories. I don't think either are expressly good for the liver but both aid the function of the bowel expressly when one is dehydrated. Both stimulate urination so either requires a lot of the stuff which can keep you hydrated or you struggle for balance. Alcohol has the byproduct of making you sweat more in the heat so it creates a cyclic neediness usually unknown to the beer drinker...they just think they are thirsty but its really the body trying to balance against dehydration. Beer like tea seem to be pretty good at flushing the kidneys which helps to avoid bladder infection as once I was actually told this by a doctor friend who learned during the war in Germany...flushing is better than no flushing...tea may be best but beer works! I don't like beer...never have. Homelessness scares me because it is ever present since we lost the family home to taxes we...none of us...could afford. I knew a homeless woman once named Gertrude who held out for coffee. She made a friend of the Christian Science Reading Room and the town square Security guards who turned a blind eye while she slept in an abandoned Japanese Restaurant. The Reading Room had a constant coffee pot but I think she dealt with dehydration as her skin always looked way too dry. The test for dehydration is to pinch the skin and the back of your hand and see how slowly it returns to normal form or to scratch your arm and see if it leaves white lines. Dehydration can make you stupid besides the physical damage it causes...your brain is 72& water. Stupid really doesn't help when you are at your wits end and trying to find what you should do...like fear it makes your mind small and you miss obvious options available to you or you think of them when its too late to act on them. I think many people who don't pay attention deal with dehydration as it sneaks up on you even when you are aware it is an issue...get focused and determined or work too long or don't notice that you have been sweating and its your problem! I have adopted the bad habit of wanting to dig my way out of this hole I'm in so badly that when I have something to do to try to succeed I can have a cup of coffee sitting beside me and I will forget to drink it until I am dehydrated. The body has a specific response to dehydration for everyone...first it retains fluids...conserves. It's all the stuff you hear about Hyper and Hypothermia. It's the cause of Heat Stroke. Electricity needs a conductor...water is one of the main conductors in your body...when the body conserves many pieces of you get less than their share of fluids so one of the first things it causes is a general numbing effect. Ok so you get dehydrated and your brain kind of ignores it then your body agrees...your survival is in jeopardy. I have never heard a good medical reason for the cause of congestive heart failure and I have asked but I do know that a substance in Robitussin is used for mountain climbers who are stranded to fight Hypothermia because fluid retention in the lungs kills. In mild forms though not less deadly it is what a doctor looks for to determine pneumonia. My mother had congestive heart failure and we watched her ankles for signs of swelling which then led to lungs that didn't move air anymore...really scary thing! The body begins retaining fluid at the first signs of dehydration...my life experience tells me to put the pieces together so you pay attention to fluid intake and waste. On the topic of good water I am a true believer in the Zero Water Filters...all it takes is a meter testing of tap water to realize we drink a lot of stuff that isn't H2O! Powdered Chlorine leaves a specific residue that when mixed with that Melamac chemical that killed a lot of pets awhile back by shutting down their kidneys...it turns out the residue only becomes harmful when heated. Bottle waters brag that they use a double filtration process some even explaining that first they chemically treat the water then steam it...the EPA barely speaks to the FDA so Melamac becomes a problem when it is added to increase the protein content of wheat flour coming out of China (they killed the businessman there that caused that problem) but no one explains the acceptable processing of water because it is cheaper and safer to transport powdered chlorine instead of using the liquid chemical that leaves no residue when processed! I don't have the luxury of the filters on a regular basis so my coffee is made with tap water. My daughter grinds her beans but I can't afford that luxury either but I can tell you it delivers more caffeine to me! I love my daughter's coffee! In Europe they are studying non-sugar cane additives to sugar and calling them empty calories yet stateside they say a sugar is a sugar and it doesn't matter where it comes from. My body seems to be able to tell the difference between the two. I get indigestion from sugar that isn't 100% cane sugar...don't know why...in a blind test it works with me. I want cane sugar but get whatever I can...that's addiction! Once upon a time I tried dieting without sugar and I can tell you my experience is that you go through a physical withdrawal when you give up sugar entirely even substituting the artificial sweeteners for it so I gave up...I drink sweet coffee! Sweetened with what I call good sugar...did I just make corporate people angry at me? Most likely but I have grown Stevia and bought it and it works on the brain part of 'sweet' without personal side effects it just doesn't boost my energy levels. When it comes to milk I'll take it any way I can get it or go without but I can tell you this...when not eating a lot you crave cholesterol and the higher the content in milk in coffee the more food like it feels especially when you are saving money by eating beans! Heaven is a cup of my daughter's coffee with whipping cream just poured in it and good sugar. I am living proof that you can survive several days of no food by just drinking coffee. It also makes aches and pain seems less defined...not as good as a pill for that purpose but it hits some receptor somewhere I think. Because of my blood pressure I also add caffeine where I can which led to instant coffee in juice...and orange is better than cranberry...trust me! I feed my body cravings and not the aesthetics of eating though I like those as well as the next guy but until my art sells or my husband gets hired...its been an education! Cravings are not only for pregnant women...ask any hungry person...they know what I mean. Like I said I am addicted to Coffee and those who love me know it and show up with a cup when they come to visit which grows less often the longer we poor people...

I lightly mentioned milk...I should say more. Milk can keep a newborn alive for 6 months without food...I think that should mean something. When in my life I have been at my least...ok, I will explain that. I grew up a girlie girl with Cinderella dreams and a strong Christian background. I got married young to a man my parents didn't approve of who was ten years my senior. My parents were right. I ended up in the hospital 6 months pregnant with dehydration and malnutrition because I 'kept only unto him' and told no one I was starving. Three days later I went home to my parent's house to be fattened up. I couldn't eat...I'd throw up. My mother dug in her bag of depression era tricks for recipes. She poached eggs and served them on toast in warmed milk with extra butter...that I could eat! That gave me strength because of the egg protein too...over time I got stronger. Soups...she put everything in soups. She made fudge a lot! Then I graduated to pasta and I swore I should give my son an Italian name because of all the spaghetti I ate! We built me up and I was fifty pounds overweight when the baby came. Eventually the preacher that married us told me to get a divorce or I wouldn't have...I quit believing in the man but not the idea of marriage...maybe you say silly me and maybe you are right but I believe in it none the less and just kept trying. So milk given at short intervals like you feed a baby can keep you breathing and your digestive track working too...that's why there are diapers for babies! It works so I try to make sure milk is in my pantry regularly though its not always easy to come by. (I have to go get the last of my orange juice with instant coffee in it just now...this isn't a work of fiction...I'm living it which is why my daughter thought I should write it I guess.) My mother was born in 1916 and grew up on an island that had no bridge before phones and television existed. She knew all kinds of really basic things because you couldn't call a doctor if you got sick very well. Her milk came from the cow they brought to the island and she even knew how to wring a chicken's neck! Really! I'm not making this up! I greatly prefer homogenized milk...the irradiated shelf stuff is great too...powdered doesn't last as long as one would hope but its a useful staple when you can get it and I love to cook with it. I avoid most creamers simply because they aren't milk and it's the same with cheeses mostly because of the usable calcium and again I bet on how I feel when I eat them and not the package. Calcium is required for the electric switches in the brain...need I say more about how important it is? When times have been really tough and say my lights are out so my daughter takes me to her house for a few days...she reminds me of milk and I eat small meals several times a day with a glass of milk with each and usually in about three days I'm almost human! I also believe in Instant Breakfast by Carnation...200 calories...all your vitamins and some protein too! In a hospital setting they keep people who can't eat alive on Ensure which is also available but is a lot more expensive and divided into types to aid people with a normal diet achieve specific health goals. Carnation created Instant Breakfast at a time in our country when corporate growth was beginning and people began to skip breakfast...it is intended to replace a meal and I think it can. Besides...if your pantry has Instant Breakfast and Powdered Milk you can survive a disaster...did I mention I live in Florida...home of the always prepared for a hurricane people! (Although for hurricane consideration it is best to store both in a water tight plastic tub that can float! Bottled water can be the least of your concern when the lights go out in a storm...) Milk and bouillon gravy make or a soup base...most any can of vegetables can become a soup! I like Calcium where I can get it too! Canned evaporated milk hits those 'feels like food' buttons when you're hungry but requires refrigeration after opening...my mother solved the water concerns by using it as part of her hurricane items and the lady I stayed with in Banff preferred it even for morning cereal but I think her reasoning was waste reduction, cost and sheer elegance in a creamer when you serve demitasse coffee after dinner. My mother drank tons of Butter Milk and Yogurt when she went through chemo because a doctor told her it could help fight Thrush...chemo reduces the immune system so they end up giving you antibiotics which can cause a Thrush response. My grandmother ate cottage cheese daily while going through radiation treatments though she never explained why...maybe she just liked it...I love it but it has a really high salt content (water balance again!). Yogurt is the definition of how important the digestive tract is...when Dannon first came to the U.S. they marketed the fact that in the Himalayas people live longer and they all eat yogurt! The ads have changed but that hasn't. In the Himalayas they also serve a goat milk drink to company that works like a meal and is reportedly heavily oiled though I haven't tried it nor do I care to but goat's milk is amazing for the skin in a lotion...feels like none other! The big fad approach to Coral Calcium also has some merit in that longevity is common in Korea and it is in the soil there so it's in everything you eat but more than that there is some research concerning calcium and its ability to inhibit cancer that's quite interesting. Milk curdles when you heat it with orange juice though so don't try that...yuck! Milk Serveche is a bad thing!!!

Spinach...first thing I learned when I worked for the Nutrition Division was that Popeye's can of Spinach was a lie! Turns out they told me that the iron in spinach is almost impossible to digest. I have also since learned that spinach is full of lots of good nutrients including calcium. Then I learned from the diet information in the 6 Day Diet that it is easily digested only to later see a science show with one of those swallowed capsule monitors that in fact it digests and excretes in 2 hours normally. Perfect for a test of your own system or to keep a system with less food functioning! I take a can of spinach, a handful of grated cheese and a chunk of butter...nuke it and make it a meal! Yum! Then 2 hours later...see? All the nutrients and a simple understanding of your body's ability to work right! It's extremely easy to grow as are Chard, Kohlrabi, and lots of other greens which remarkably look just as nice as a fern in a pot...leaf lettuce isn't so pretty but more readily accessed in that you don't have to wait for the plant to fully mature to eat it. Green onions are simply a must as they never spoil in the fridge...pull one/plant one...easy and fresh! I love sprouts too. Fresh greens carry something unusual with them...Nicotinic acid! You will find for all the conversation about the poison nicotine (and it can be) that Nicotinic Acid (read your B vitamin labels!) is required by the body...it fights cholesterol...its the secret ingredient in erection enhancers! Now there is a balance issue with taking the supplement that isn't well known but I learned the hard way...when you quit taking large doses of Nicotinic Acid your Triglycerides soar and you can develop Gout or in my case Gouty Arthritis apparently. When I think landscaping a yard, I think edible ornamentals in most all the perennial beds and why not? Growing plants survive disaster better than say refrigerated ones and you should always boil them if water supply has been questionable but they are still edible! A storm may wash away the dirt but the plant remains edible for some time! Potatoes make elegant hanging baskets as do Tomatoes (which require lime for an acid soil to produce fruit!) which vine naturally and Peas climb a hanger as does Malabar Spinach that grows like a weed and tastes better than grocery store...it even reseeds itself if you let the flowers lay on the ground after bloom making it virtually free food! I have never gotten to grow a yard my way but have tried everything to include my current Egg Plants and Peppers. (Turns out you have to spend a couple of months in England to add Feng Shui to Edible Ornamental Gardener and a Horticultural degree to get a job in this field...tried though even giving up my taste in variety to learn local flowering varieties but nowadays people just want their grass cut and big things hauled off which I don't think I could do consistently!) Sprouts are amazing and you even get the Niacin flush if you are deficient but I learned 2 things: First seeds can get moldy over time and secondly, water quality matters so in a poor household you may not be able to store seeds and grow good edible sprout. On the up side I have a friend who had bypass surgery and needed fresh greens so I talked him into doing it on his desk at work! He loves it! You get a layered tray set (Sprout People.com is where I go because they have really good cheap seed and the trays!) but don't try to stock pile seed. Be sure when you cook dried beans to always soak them overnight with no salt in the water literally looking for them to begin to sprout before cooking them and you can get the sprout effect from a pot of beans. Guys need Nicotinic Acid...fresh greens...or they can just wait and get the little blue pill but watch out for arthritis later... Japanese vegetables are on a similar longitude to our northern areas and are currently doing well in the north east...family gardens feed people. Picking the Tomato that grows like a weed in say Mexico to try in Florida is my point of view. It's a thought... My patio is pretty and there is food there too!

Downturned corners of a mouth that sometimes look chapped and pink are signs of iron deficiency. Raisins not only increase Iron in your system but also increase appetite when someone has little or no appetite. Some people swear by canned Sardines to increase iron too...both work pretty quickly...

Chapped lips are significant of Pancreas deficiency...the outer edge of your tongue being red is Lung...a white coat on your tongue is digestive difficulties where a black spot shows long term illness according to TCM. Taoist exercises explained later correct tongue diagnosis issues. They say eyes and nails are governed by the Liver but feet hurting is also attributed to Liver.

My experience agrees with experts that say Biotin added to your diet improve the growth of nails and hair. I have found Keratin the best type of shampoo with Mill Creek first ordering it on the market if you can find that brand.

My grandmother taught me that you check blood pressure by pinching a finger tip and seeing how quickly it turns pink again long before they developed those fancy clips they put on your fingers at hospitals. She also taught me a blue ring around your lips is symptomatic of oxygen in the blood while grey or white lips are significant of heart issues.

To warm yourself in cold weather you pant rapidly like a dog...this works!.

Can goods during disasters of any kind are a saving grace. No water...there's usually juice in the can. No electricity? Cold food is food but a can can be used as a pot over a fire. They survive most anything...you don't use them as much when you can do better so they tend to still be there when you need them. Canned fruit can add vitamin C which is essential especially when health issues are a concern like weather or bad sanitation situations Canned meats are protein when you need it...your condiments may go, unless you normally store excess in plastic tubs which I don't because my needs so far are financial not naturals disaster but I should because I live in Florida (my family thinks me weird enough...to go that far would just worry them but maybe not...my daughter has started storing stuff in plastic containers I have noted recently...hmmm...). I use a hand can opener as habit and they still work when the lights go off...

Chocolate is a pretty good pain reliever if you can get it. I always wondered about the war stories where the soldier brought stockings and chocolate bars to get a girl like they were always available. They sound like friendly things to do and nylons certainly have their uses but why would soldiers have easy access? (By the way my brother the nuclear physicist taught me that if you put nylons and nail polish with nylon in it in the freezer it strengthens the nylon and your hose will last longer as will your manicure!) Hot chocolate with red pepper in it makes a wonderful drink! I believe I got that from a historical show on Aztecs but I have tried it and remarkably it increases your endorphins and relieves aches and pains pretty well! I also sneak chocolate in to meals I cook... M&M's are my friends!

My husband has a passion for ice cream...I insist on chocolate and tell myself it is a calcium source then use it with my Instant Breakfast. Ice Cream costs about the same as a gallon of milk the way we buy it but it lasts longer because after all Ice Cream is a treat! I can tell you when the water goes off it is wise to use one cup and spoon each and quickly put it in the fridge between uses which saves washing bowls. I can tell you 20 seconds in the microwave and you have a terrific milk shake or soft serve Ice Cream...and I can tell you its yummy with chocolate Instant Breakfast for many useful reasons...turns a treat into a meal!

Honey has become expensive and they say bees are doing weird things these days but it has amazing uses to include antibacterial properties and wound healing. The old confederate use of a spider web on a wound leaves a black mark but honey can do almost as well. Herbally? Arnica is for bruises...Valerian for sore muscles...Mistletoe or All Heal as it used to be called is an anti yeast infection herb. Wiping someone down with Vinegar and water can break even the worst fever I think better than an ice bath. I could go on but Not trying to practice medicine here as I am not qualified and these are just results from my experience...of course an herbal knowledge and how to make teas, salves, ointments and tinctures is always a useful skill for survival and recognizing them in the wild is the real skill. I am only barely qualified to say I know anything useful!

 I figure if I put enough useful stuff in here my book might sell! A girl's gotta try right?

Making yourself eat a can of peas for a couple of days because you weren't stocked is a psychological personal war...you look at the lights around you as we choose to live in a complex rather than isolated and you know they aren't eating Peas today for sustenance. That's part of the living hell stuff I mentioned earlier but over time it becomes your norm. You simply wonder if this is what you deserve in life and you don't have those feelings of being picked on which is where I am. Apartments are safer and smarter in my opinion because there are people nearby who would hollar for help if you need it. Also with neighbors you can say offer to take their trash out for a week to get your phone charged...we have done that as well as making friends with the nearby convenient store people who might charge your phone when your lights are out too...isolation would be much worse. Distance becomes an issue when you say have a car but it isn't legal so you won't drive it but if you needed to get to a hospital its still there until they take the tag away that is...this is what current insurance laws cause. Recently we had above ground gas storage tanks at a gas station blow up down the road from us and as I spoke to my daughter some 40 miles away at work we debated what would happen. They evacuated everyone from a block away from us on and all I could think of was that in the Wild West they shot people who stole horses because transportation could mean life or death...kind of dropped into that hell place for the duration of the threat you know? First we knew of what had happened our lights went out...the whole area had no lights unexpectedly! Now the last time our lights went off was because a Charity that said they would pay our bill which becomes an issue every few months as you can only juggle for so long did not make the payment on time so next time we asked for an extension the light company refused meaning it would be 2 weeks before we could pay and no lights until then. We didn't need this time too... Weirdly when money is tight and you are trying you learn to live in the dark alot anyway but when you didn't do anything wrong and they go off it feels different. When there's a crisis like this it feels one way and when it's weather it feels different still...its funny really. I used to live by candle light when younger raising children so much so after my kids were asleep the neighbors knew which room I was in by where they saw the candle...I heated by fireplace...all things to save money so I could spend it on the kids. I do not do that now though I should I suppose but the feeling is you have to draw a line in the sand somewhere and I'm just not a refuge...then the news says we are headed for a double dip depression...things are expected to get worse...

Someone should think about what happens when the lights go out. First if you don't have ready cash to buy ice, frozen food is garbage and sooner better than later to dispose of it...trust me! The weather outside is now inside only without circulation. Time stands still except for battery clocks. The world goes silent. For us there becomes nothing to do but wait as we live on computer for one reason or another. There can be no applications put in...no replies by email...no new art on Zazzle...we're just dead in the water. There are no meals...we don't have a bbq even though a Hibachi would be more my choice and they are almost impossible to find these days and ridiculously expense for a simple means to cook safely on an open fire. Your first thought is to cook off the frozen goods if you can't buy ice and to let someone besides yourself know while you still have a phone only you can't cook and you know no one you call can do anything about it because of course you tried to ask for help to keep the lights on. I have just resorted to a family email with the words lights are off...why says anything else? Then you sit and consider how helpless you are. Ok that's what you do when you half way have you life such that it is basically disrupted by the event. Basically...survivally...there's what you can do and what you just can't so you then just sit. You wonder how far this will undo everything you have worked towards, you know? You consider lost momentum and bad timing issues but mostly you just sit. Can't use the phone to save for emergency then at night you sit in the dark or by candle to save batteries you can't replace in camp lamps. I have tinnitus since my wreck so bad that I go to tears without some noise so there has to be a radio going for me... Three days and the fight or flight chemicals are released but there's nowhere to go. 2 weeks is an incredibly long time...to just sit...I sleep days...not so much in the Florida heat...I work nights while my husband sleeps...he sleeps I sit since I can't work. Cyber space is the holder of my published stuff...that brings peace of mind as it is still for sale somewhere while I sit... I made it three days before my husband found a way to charge the phone and my daughter came and got us. Turns out she had been so worried about us she was half sick over it and glad to get us to her house so it isn't just us that got affected. She and her husband put off a bill with us promising to pay them back at the end of 2 weeks all the while knowing if we didn't make it through the electricity shut off the water would follow. We paid them back...the water goes today...I have juice because she bought it for me and instant coffee because we tried to be prepared. And today I write!

Food Stamps are the one good thing that came from losing our house. Couldn't get them and own property. Food Stamps mean I don't have to call my daughter and admit I'm hungry and beg food. I have transferred my old promise to my mother that I would never starve again without telling someone to her and she readily brings me food whether its from her kitchen or a store. She knows how I live...she checks my fridge when she visits...she knows I don't want her money too but she has promised she won't let me starve. She is raising my 2 grandsons and shouldn't spend money on anything else! I hate making that phone call. She's coming today. Food stamps do not buy toilet paper or bleach which is a necessity especially when the water goes off but also to clean refrigerators after you throw away your food. There will be no showers or laundry until its back on. I should run take a quick shower now but my back hurts and I'm too tired just now see I have hair to my waist that has to be brushed to wash it and that is hard for me. All this is going to cost me my hair...I am so vain! You wash all your dishes and bleach your counters. You fill all your containers and fill the tub for flushing toilets. $60 or ten days without water...food stamps come tomorrow! Eventually your world becomes wrapped around such things. I hope my daughter is right about writing my story eventually making money...I am tired of this. It could be so much worse I know but I am not in great health and its really really hard...

I met a woman in Toronto who was wife of a family friend I visited all those years ago coming back from Banff. Her husband wanted to take us all out for Mc Donalds...she called him aside and plans were changed to eat burgers at home and she made me my first Rhubarb Pie to soften the blow of not going out. I asked him the next day why she got so squirrely about a trip to Mc Donalds and he thought about it and all he could say was 'she lived through the depression'. I thought to myself, 'God! I hope I never become her'. I wonder today if I have...

I just ate for three days on a regular sized can of whole potatoes cubed, a dill pickle diced, and a small can of tuna making, with mayo and mustard, a terrific salad! Of course there were Instant Breakfasts, a couple of sandwiches and a couple of ounces of cheese too...who-hoo! All the good stuff!

Homeless people almost never get to wash their hands in warm water...I think of that every time I wash my hands in warm water with a little thank you God for a roof and electricity too...everyone should do that I think...those who have warm water to wash in that is...

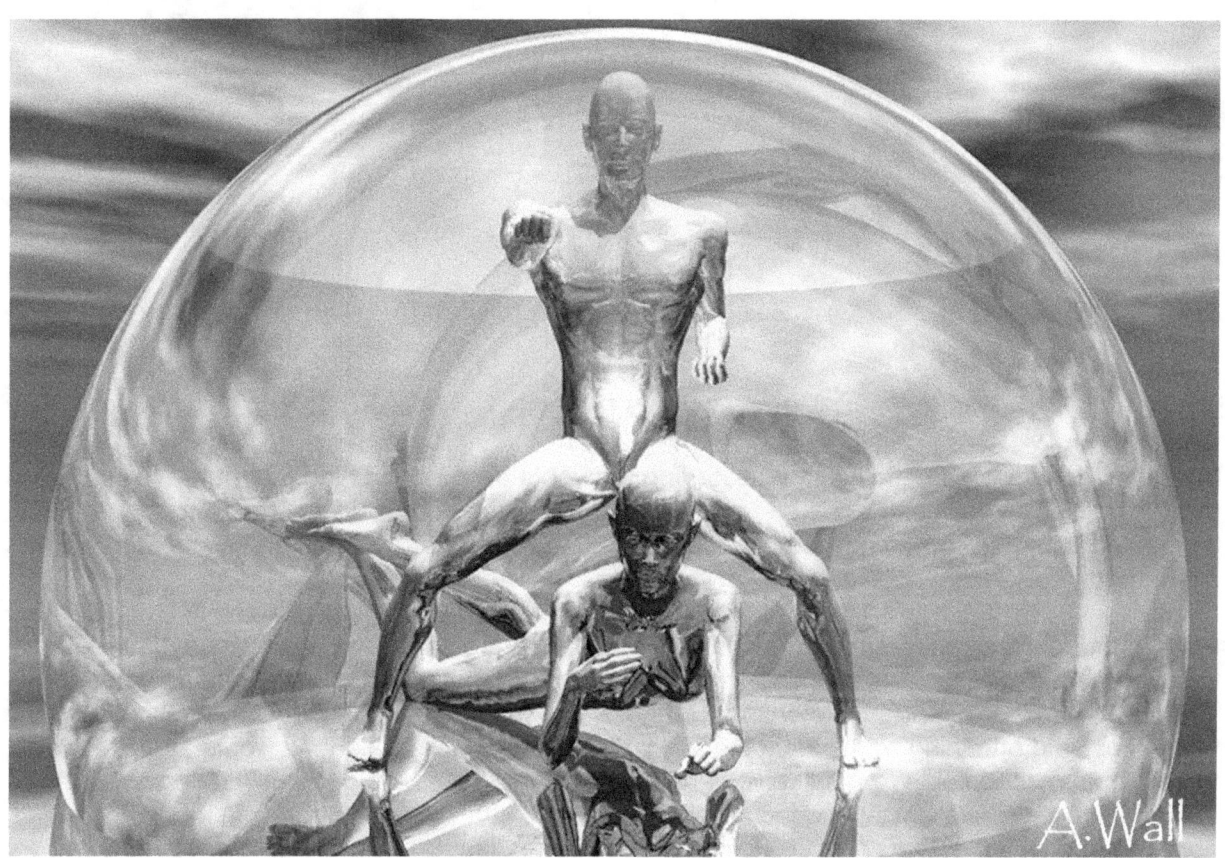

~ CHAPTER FOUR ~

My days and nights sometimes shift according to events but working nights are always kinder to me. Transition periods of all kids are rough. The Great Napoleon said circumstances change things and I change circumstances...of course he also said an army fights on its stomach...what did he know?

I raised four children with one predominate principle...we are known by what we say and do in this world. The idea is that you should always be sure to mean what you say and do what you say you will do. I demanded straight answers but always allowed emotional outbursts. I worried when they said one thing and did another or did not do what they said they would as both trying to hold them accountable to themselves and using what I see as the good psychology of routing out things that get in the way of accomplishing personal goals no matter how small. I began college twice with the goal of a psychology degree in mind later having to drop out but if you want to learn something you study anyway and what I learned from everything I read is that the entire field can be boiled down to this idea. If you do not know what you mean there is a problem...if you let things interfere with accomplishing your goals...there is a problem. My theory was to cut to the chase and just start there. Think of it...you never have to say you will do things you don't intend to do or you are fooling someone...yourself or someone else...and there are always reasons when you do that explain deeper meanings of what is going on with you. Reasons like peer pressure...expectations that aren't based on fact...deliberate deception again for reasons are all symptoms of psychological problems in my opinion so I started with a simple principle they could never say they didn't understand and the rest would come out and be dealt with as they occurred. It could be frustrating to a child (or adult?) so I had no problem with proper expression of anger...again another issue people deal with when older. They could yell at me without reprisal and sometimes I found what they would shout at the top of their lungs was what they really felt and meant...I always listened. I even once taught my daughter primal screaming face first into a sink full of water so as not to scare the neighbors somewhere after the argument where she stomped upstairs yelling at the top of her lungs...'It Isn't Hormones!', which she still laughs about today. At the time she had been angry that I actually listened to what she said that made little sense but moreover the angst with which she said it and she was the right age. Now that she knows what hormones are she has said I was probably right...the one thing my kids have always hated about me...too often Mama was right! This was a standard I could live by having caught on early that children learn most from the example you set. This is the principle I use in business and even today in life. I would rather tell you that I can't do something than lie and later let you down. If you look at the record keeping we are currently being judged by this is the predominate factor. Did you do what you said you would? If you didn't you can't be trusted and aren't dependable...can you say credit history and criminal background check? Can you also say why these things need to be done in the first place? Even now I am pleased I raised them this way however deception runs rampant in our society...

The worst part of being poor is being forced to break your word. You say you will do things and circumstances change and you just can't. Personally it makes me afraid to sound confident on most anything. Betting on an extension of the electric bill as per their rules, we got an extension on the water bill...we didn't know the charity hadn't paid what they said they would on time. The cure made us lie to the water company. Now that violates a fundamental principle of 'self' I have always lived by! The very order of a couple of phone calls...the very nature of getting charity I suppose where you have to be grateful for help on their terms but a utility company doesn't has shaped my outcome. As a responsible person I have a real problem saying it wasn't my fault. I have to say I don't think it was but we could have found out somehow about the electric bill before making arrangements with the water company if we had known...we didn't know. This is the misconception of what is going on in the business world today I think...see we will be judged by these events won't we...

The other value I passed on to my children is the idea of 'learning' and why one would want to. If you are the stupid person in a group...you get treated like you are stupid and people take advantage of you...so you need to know...you need to teach yourself so you aren't that guy! If my kids were that guy I held them accountable for it of course this also taught me what they didn't know and I would make an opportunity for them to learn what they didn't know! It was a good thing and what I hoped would be a lifelong ideal. The other thing I had to argue with the school system about is the idea that you 'have' to be in a school setting to learn! That industry has become so self propagating that children no longer know that when they wake up and open their eyes...they are in fact learning! The other thing is how you learn. If you can read and understand what you read...must you be taught? I can see needing guidance on where to find what you want to learn and someone to answer questions that you do not understand but you do not need a translator for a book if you can read...that's what dictionaries are for! Kids in school today don't know that. They believe that if someone doesn't tell them someone else's interpretation of words on a page...they haven't learned what a book has to offer! What a great loss to our society! I tried to unravel these issues with my kids but as they have grown, Mama is a weirdo and society knows how to be. I have gotten fussed at for explaining to grands how the school system works or teasing them about 'choosing' to not be the smartest kid in class though I hope I motivated a little real education by saying those things.

It's a dilemma when I am being forced to live by rules I agree with all the while being turned into the guy who can't keep his word! I look like I don't believe in the very rules I taught my children to observe! I am more self educated than school educated and no one believes that is possible! I have walked miles to get a book I wanted to read...I have walked miles to keep an appointment too. Today I do not walk so well and cannot do these things so I am at the mercy of others who do not necessarily hold my standard. Now being on time never mattered to me as much as the guy on the tight schedule except when I have been the guy on the tight schedule...but isn't that how that always works? If I say I will be there I will...but sometimes I have to walk and may be late... Today timing means more than ever before and order of events can cut off your utilities and not knowing things that can't be learned by normal means can make a liar of you. I can understand what confuses my children...

I have heard whispered in my ear that my sons Bachelor Party is coming soon...knowing when I have begun checking the items I designed for him for that event. Three days before the function and filled with hope I have sold nothing. All my kids swear they like what I designed, swear they want me on my feet, how much they hate me going through hard times, how me making a living is their fondest goal and I am sure someone will tell me they couldn't be afforded...then they will tell me how much money they spent to have a good time... The worst part is if I do not smile through it all they simply quit telling me anything. This happens all the time...

During the course of having four children and several marriages, financial management changes from ideas of college and career plans to what to do now? Throw in that a first husband never supported his child...none of the fathers did more than the minimum...child support concerns become part of your budget concept. You don't spend money that isn't yours to spend and under the careful watchful eye of ex-husbands, family services and your own children...there are lots of things you just don't do for yourself. Now as matter of course their diet was foremost in my concern...cheap balanced nutrition was the name of the game and the recipes they grew up on were based on that concept. From 1974 until 1997 when I threw up my hands and told my children if they wanted me to cook they would give me a clean kitchen to do it in so the youngest two learned how to cook! The average meal size for dinner were recipes for ten...growing boys have hollow legs...I had three! You just don't drink the milk its for the babies...you only occasionally eat fruit because they need it more and so on. Then there are family outings...kids should have certain memories as adults. When just my two oldest and me it was Dollar Movie Night with hot dogs because they were cheap...kept that up even to when I was the neighborhood chauffer taking a car load and picking them up after. Sleep overs...there were rules for those...only on Saturday Night with advance warning so extra places could be set for the regular Saturday Spaghetti...see you can feed a crowd cheaply on spaghetti. When I was married there were a few trips to Disney with the kids...twice I think that I got to go but I sent them every school trip or daddy vacation that came along and once a year the Fair came to town but we ended up not going for several years in the early 90's because there just wasn't enough money. Dating was a sneaky thing I did after my oldest tried to sell me to a date once to get a new dad. I never went far or often though. I have never been lots of places but that's what you do when you have to account for every penny always...living at the beach was the one really kool thing I did that I enjoyed. My point is I think my kids think I did it wrong and have planned on getting to do all kinds of kool stuff before they get tied down. This would explain the later ages for marriage and so on. It would also explain why one kid has done New Year's in Times Square...another liked jumping out of airplanes...the ones with kids do the beach as often as they can and water parks. I had less time it seems to worry about what I was missing it seems because I had aging parents and work and more often than not only me to baby sit so kids in tow. Living like that you don't miss stuff because you are too busy but looking back? I normally didn't shop for clothes for me unless I caught a Rummage Sale in my size...no haute couture for me. I think there are more kool things to do now a days than when my kids were growing up and I am delighted they haven't missed a lot. One son even hiked part of the grand canyon and another snow boards! Ain't that kool! The point is I have limited entertainment in my historic portfolio because everything else was more important...this is why I find myself wondering where I fit in, in the great scheme of things. I have no regrets...I'd do it again that way...I don't know that my kids would...maybe they are smarter than me...

People do what they really want to do. You stop learning you start dying...

Maybe they are proving Mama wrong...who knows!

I have a particular problem with the phrase 'don't give me a guilt trip'. Since when did your feelings become something someone could give you? I get beat up with that phrase by my kids when I say my water is off for example and in all honesty I think it someone's personal denial of the reality they see before them. I did it one way and my kids don't agree...then exactly why would they feel guilty and much less blame it on me? Maybe this is significant of their deep seeded plan to have the regrets I don't have when later they compare our lives...I certainly hope not but that is my best guess. I lived my life as I did for many reasons and one of them was so I wouldn't have regrets later. The only guilt I am truly familiar with as a haunting experience is survivor guilt...maybe I could have done more to help someone...you know? If only I had known then what I know now things might have been better and someone I cared for might have lived longer...the equivalent response from half the world the day after cancer is cured no doubt! My water is off was NOT my intention to make someone who likes to have a good time feel guilty but it will ever make me question their values...NO GUILT TRIPS! Some concern knowing they will outlive me about how they will feel after I am gone...now THAT worries me sincerely! Eventually I will quit trying to get my kids to do like I did...I actually cut them off from advice when they marry. My mother said...a son is a son 'til he finds him a wife but a daughter is a daughter for the rest of her life'. I even cut my daughter off from the advice mill in me but I do worry about later...I hope they will be as lucky as me with few regrets....POVERTY FREAKING KILLS! Now you know why I try so hard to survive it...   Think of it...say one day they find me dead from heat stroke and my lights were off and people knew but went on the planned vacation instead...now that could mess up someone's head! I don't want that so I just keep making it work...and they keep having fun...let us hope I can keep it up forever. At my low moments I do ask them to help please...if I was a bigger woman I would not but I can be a wuss at times...poverty is also scary if you are the realist who knows things can go south against your best effort... Once upon a time I drove a cab...had a buddy feeding a family for all that he was worth and he was incredibly skinny so I used to buy a bag of burgers and swear I was full so he would take them...in other words I fed him...doughnuts anything I could talk him into even learning to work his side of town because he worried me...then came the day they found him dead in his cab and it wasn't homicide which can happen to cab driver so they put out notices when it does. I will always wonder if I had tried harder to feed the man because I had been really busy and not seen him for a few days...ya know? I have to live with that...guilt trip? No... Reality...yes! I once didn't come when my mother asked me to, to help her move my father back into bed...told her I had to work...I had kids...the normal stuff...so she moved him and broke her back...this is guilt...what guilt trip? I would not wish such memories for my children.

You live you learn...right?

I don't know that that is true on the large scale. I listen to the news and realize that people lie to themselves entirely too often to learn from their life's experience in any meaningful way. President Obama actually understands to some degree what I am writing here. Steve Jobs who died today understands the heart of an artist when he says stay hungry and stay foolish and I have no doubt he died at peace with himself clearly admitting that no one ever wants to go. It is the people who do not understand this book that I am referring to. There is a Mr. Cain running for President who says simply if you aren't rich it is your own fault. What an ungrateful, narrow minded wretch of a man he must be! Did you hear in that statement the slightest bit of gratitude? I say narrow minded because however that man made his money...it came from people unless he manufactured it in his basement but he obviously has forgotten them all. I certainly want him in the White House so he can further push the Constitution out of his way and get serious about turning America into the money making business he thinks it should be! That last statement came with as much sarcasm as I could muster mind you. What the heck is that man doing wanting to become a servant to the public? He doesn't even understand the problem! That's right...being part of the problem it IS really hard to understand you are doing anything wrong, right? People buy products...people invest in stocks...people put money in banks so they can invest it (rolled over laughing at the Bank of America saying they have to charge $5 a person for using a debit card because they have the right to make money as though the billions banks invest of our money they hold just don't make enough!. Did you see the movie Happy-ness? It shows a man having really hard times with his son. It does not show the Social Worker sweeping in immediately taking his son to higher ground which is a more realistic story...of course he was reported by the day care worker watching his son while she finds out where they sleep and how little they eat...that could have changed everything couldn't it? It didn't show the intervention of the Security Guard at the Bus Station who had him arrested for trespassing where his son finally ended up in foster care and his career totally tossed because he was just absent for days without explanation or they found out where he was...no...would not have made a good story. Now the real problem I have isn't all that but the end result of the man who considers himself self made when he owes his entire success to that guard who probably knew he was there but did nothing...or the baby sitter who turned a blind eye while he broke laws! That movie didn't convince me anyone could do what he did...it convinced me that people make the world go round and he should be the most grateful man on the planet that he pulled off what he pulled off...he was just a good con artist! In that movie he didn't call the police when his machine was stolen. That wasn't because he didn't have the right...it was because he didn't want his story known by officials. He assaulted the bum! Again...no cops because bums don't get that luxury...they end up hauled in the minute they can't produce a valid address! I especially loved the part where he fixed a medical device for measuring bone density by hall light at a homeless shelter after shoving people out of his way to get himself in because he thought the rules didn't apply to him! Then he took that same machine and sold it to a Doctor who would then use it on idiot people like me who had no idea the history of the machine being used! I am due for a bone density test of about six months ago...whew...no insurance meant no test but where do they get all those machines and where were they first? My future could be determined by such a test and that movie will always make me wonder if medical tests can be trusted or will people like that man who thanked no one get elected President? He broke all the rules but he made a movie...is it possible that people would vote for the celebrity and not see the crime of his success? Do we live and learn or are we so battered by poverty that it just seems people with money all know something we don't so they must be worshipped? I think it's nuts! I envision a painting of the last supper with the current Tea Party and RNC leadership sitting at a table with their chosen scape goat...doesn't that sound like art to you?

The three day notice for my rent turned up on my door today on schedule. I have the best landlord in the world to split my rent as they do and work with me or I would not have a roof or utility bills to worry about! I am grateful...let me publish that here and should I ever become successful unlike the politicians I hear on TV...I will remember who helped me succeed!!!

Current events...learned today one of my grands got bitten by a brown recluse...no one called because there is nothing I can do to help but they did post it on their wall at Facebook! They caught the snipers in California but not the 2 lose where my son and daughter live but not to worry...it's not like the DC Sniper the kids tell me. I beat my daughter in the Words scrabble game so we started a new one today. Thank goodness my brain is still working!

Helplessness...it has an effect over time. I worked Security among other myriad jobs of the life of a wife who follows her husband and tries to add to the income but Security was a real career choice I thought. Like the guys in the legal shows on TV you learn an odd practice of dividing your thinking. There is what you know you saw...what you need to say to explain it in terms of legalities to employers...and what you say to normal people who don't normally see such things or understand them. It produces that cynical look that makes a cop stand out in a crowd...it once cost me dinner but I'll explain that later. I think cops carry weapons mostly because they know the kinds of things they will see and they have to live long enough to report it to someone else but there are those cops who carry a gun because it makes them feel powerful. Powerful people like helpless people because it allows their self image to continue...how can they possibly see themselves as powerful without them? How can superior people see themselves as superior without a good bunch of inferior people to daunt over? (A cast system right here in America.) Poor people divide their thinking too...it is wise to act helpless when dealing with powerful people...stupid when dealing with people who think themselves smart and so on...you might get a handout if you let them see you as the lesser soul. I am NOT good at this tactic of poverty. I spent too many years being the stupid seeming woman so people would like me...a trick you learn if you have a brain as a child. Grown ups do not like truly smart children! How can you parent when they catch your mistakes? You do it naturally then you realize what you have done and how it worked then you do it deliberately...then you just get tired and do it because its easiest... If this is you then you know what I mean when I say you have a natural inclination towards security work because unlike enforcement you see trends and potentials and all you have ever wanted was the right to tell people before bad things happen and actually be heard. Security people make people safer. But who listens to poor people who are some of the best observers in the world as they have both time and reason to watch people. Helplessness isn't not knowing...its a matter of not even being in the game. It's called disenfranchisement or politically sidelining an opponent. The deal is to make someone a person who doesn't know what's going on so they become ineffective...it wins elections! I happen to know from my own experience that if you can beat someone in an election whether you ever considered running or not...you can be made helpless deliberately. Then there is simply cascading events and coincidence that can sink your boat. It doesn't matter what made you helpless to begin with...what matters is what you do about it. Some people do absurd things to get someone to listen to them...they call that acting out when dealing with children...they call it a cry for help when dealing with someone suicidal...they called it going postal when its and angry ex-employee...all kinds of names for the same thing. They call it being a mother who has too many questions and opinions when your children are grown and its simply easier to keep her stupid. I never taught my children this trick. Where did they learn it?

They learned it from me. Selflessness means thinking other people's problems are more important than your own. I set that bad/good example and now I have to live with it. They are debating the issue I think as they gave up a lot for me to be that way. I gave up a lot too...why should I be surprised that later in life when I want to quit being that way, I don't get to. Why would I be surprised that they want to quit being selfless after the childhoods I gave them? It all really makes sense but it isn't necessarily fun for me. I am willing to recognize what I did to myself...there is no need for forgiveness...I hope they are smarter than me! I could be sidetracked easily by things in someone else's life if in the bigger picture the issue was more important and they always seemed to be to me. I never strived to earn a fortune. I am not making excuses for my behavior just stressing that there is a balance to be maintained here that should be clearly better thought out than the effort I put forth. My thought was a difficult childhood leads to tremendous coping and problem solving skills so I was excused at not being more selfishly a guard of our finances and time. Maybe I hurt their feelings in the process or maybe they just feel that everyone was more important to me than they were and its just my turn to deal with it. Either way...we as a family are the result of the choices I made and I honestly have no regrets...it's just hard. My mother once called the life she shared with me as the state of living from one crisis to another and I swore that would not be the life I gave my kids but they will tell you we lived from crisis to crisis in their memory...

I used to run what outsiders called a small democracy with my kids. When it was dinner time everyone got heard. I created a framework in which we functioned and conversation and opinion filled in the squares of what was important to do with extraordinary opportunities always taking the lead. When everyone is heard in a family there is no reason to fake stupidity and loads of reasons to be smarter than the other guy just to get to do what you want! When it was just 2 kids at home and me, this became the dinner caucus...so I would say 'what will we have tonight?' then the debate would ensue...what do we need to eat and why...what can we afford and why...what timing would allow and why...what we really wanted and why...by the time we all agreed and it was decided, everybody was really hungry and we enjoyed the heck out of the meal. My kids have some of the finest minds I have ever known! I trust their decision making and try to stay current to keep up. I never wanted to be a helpless tagalong in their lives...then comes money and its effects. You tell yourself they just don't have time for you...that's what you tell yourself...

I am opinionated...I know I am. Here I have expressed opinions I normally would not because to find them someone actually had to read this book and that means they want my opinions...I don't know why my daughter thinks anyone would do that but this book was her idea. I even asked her straight up if writing a book was her idea of giving me busy work to keep me out of her hair and she swears that's not it. (Hey...there is a wedding going on and no one has allowed my involvement as nothing I made has sold! Don't understand that either!) I really don't know what I think about her suggesting this but I am being honest here and I imagine some of my kids will have opinions about that if they ever get to read this so maybe I should apologize in advance if I hurt anyone's feelings. Distance may make the heart grow fonder...familiarity may breed contempt...but I say poverty leads to utter confusion when you have time on your hands and all the rules change right before your eyes. I know how I raised my kids...I know I feel helpless now...

They see me work. My daughter expressly has seen me work on the rare occasions of visits to her house...I don't stop...how can I take time off? I haven't gotten ahead yet! I have made her look at the products I have for sale and she tells me they are great...even my daughter-in-law had to admit she likes some of the shoes I have designed. I have turned my grand kids into cartoon characters so their parents should want those products...right? No... My friend who is up to his ears in anime and Star Wars regalia nods and smiles at my stuff...but no one buys! They have money for Star Bucks...money for lunches at Red Lobster...and pity for me. I am seen as a Problem though I work more in a day than a lot of them...my family and friends...and my husband certainly works harder at taking care of us no matter which current poverty issue we deal with as he tries to get work. People know I am trying every day. How am I the helpless one...the problem...the issue to be resolved?

My intention is to explore the pieces and parts of my circumstance and the thoughts surrounding it...mine and those I hear...to frame the useful information of the art of survival in hopes someone can tell me how in America you can work this hard surrounded by those who love you and be this helpless! I just don't get it... Should artists starve because they are artists?

Hey...maybe they should! Maybe people don't want to look in the mirror of someone else's eyes and see themselves...maybe it frightens them...maybe they find no value in someone else's opinion. If I hadn't sold my art before I would blame my skill level but I have made a living selling my art historically...that can't be it or at least I tell myself that (like all artists I am as insecure as the next guy and ever unsure! I am certainly doing more personal work today than I have done before. If I listened to that concept I would quit producing...lose inspiration...I can't do that.) I keep trying to improve my work which for me means learning the computer programs I work with better and I learn new tricks every day. I have taken my inspiration from the worlds my children and friends live in so I know the topics are current...I'm not trying to sell a perspective they don't agree with...ie: they love their child and I turn them into super hero cartoon characters! (That was the little boy bitten by a spider today...he does not own a T-shirt with his character on it...the same approach worked for Disney...hello Mickey!) I produce objects people will buy every day...T-Shirts...Coffee Mugs...designer sneakers (made by Keds)...mouse pads...invitations...hats...not just the canvas version of art though I produce those too hoping that will encourage sales...the pricing is not ridiculous either.

There are people who cannot read and write graduating from high school every year who find jobs. Your guess is as good as mine why my husband who has worked in the computer industry since almost the first Sinclair before his first Commodore...was commended in the military for computer work he did there...has a two year electronics degree and who has a book full of best employee commendations from both America On Line and Comcast...cannot find a job. He even looks pretty and downright handsome in a suit which he isn't afraid to wear. Blindfolded he can teach people over a phone how to trouble shoot their own computer and they in turn historically recommended him for those commendations! Why is he not employed? He is current with changes in his field...knows all the pc os's...and all the current video games too! He puts in 6 hours a day applying...staying current...last interview where he thought he had a job he was told the guy wanted someone he could train??? What does that mean?? Our best guess was he was over qualified...which means what? Perhaps a boss would fear for his own job? To us that job would have meant an end to a nightmare...my husband has applied to be a janitor at Wal-Mart too! It is not that he won't take any job...they won't hire him! The appearance to those around is that he isn't trying hard enough...won't take a lesser job...and the toll it takes on the soul of a man is to know this is what people think and have to argue to himself that he is no bum... It is his war too this argument I am turning into a book. My husband is a good guy! He would take care of his family if he could and I know this because he has for many years...my kids know this too. Sometimes I think they mourn the loss of us in full stature because we were always there for them and now for no apparent reason we just aren't...what can you do with that? We try harder every day hoping to get back there...that's what you do...

Nobody quit working because they have no job...they just quit getting paid for it! Is the system really working when everything is done by computer but it doesn't seem to be the way to make money? How many are unemployed in America? 14 million I heard today...what are they all working at every day? I actually think that is a pretty fair question...14 million Americans have been given busy work...14 million Americans aren't paying taxes...14 million Americans are tied up every day with the concerns in this book...14 million Americans are not being heard and certainly aren't working elections but 14 million Americans will find their way to the polls to vote. You don't need a job for that!

Rich, poor, young or old...my dinner table allowed everyone to have a say in what went on in their lives then as a group caring about each other we decided what was important and why...sometimes it was to benefit one of us and sometimes it was to benefit all of us but never was it keep one of us from doing what they wanted to because no one cared about their happiness or well being. The framework was there just like it is in America...the American family has become dysfunctional...

The unemployed are not scapegoats or problem children...are we? We are being portrayed in the press as accidents of a system that cannot stop itself. The system isn't the problem...democracy works but not when the halls of our governing bodies are filled with viciousness...ever have dinner when everyone was mad at each other? Boy you get a lot of good conversation and insight at that meal! Maybe once the entire world gets shoved through the cocooning stage of the computer era people will come out and see the sun and remember roses smell really good and even notice they have neighbors instead of discovering them when medical alerts or tragedy put sirens outside their door...we peek on disconnect day to see who else is like us by the tags they hang on the doors...we aren't alone even in our own complex but passing conversation never goes there. Maybe it's time someone admitted reality...why should guys with lifelong pensions care about their jobs? They got theirs...if you were smart you'd get yours too! To heck with serving the public...that's just what you say so you can get your pension! Hey...if I had been a Congressman...I would not be hurting today...all you have to do is get elected once...I say those are the problem children in our family...the system never promised Congress pensions...they gave that to themselves...then they fight over extending unemployment and who they will let in their clubhouse next...

Speaking of current events I might add that Steve Jobs died today...know I mentioned that before but it should be noted that with all the wealth and ability to seek out varied and sundry approaches to fighting his health problem and with the self stated point of view that no one wants to die...Steve Jobs died today. Plans cannot protect people from the inevitable. Lightening just turned off my lights and then turned them back on...fortunately I hit save regularly and lost nothing! Read my book...its good stuff to know! Don't think Congress is on the same page...

Oh and the old adage that Charity begins at home carries weight. In 1999 for Halloween I dressed as Lady Godiva and went bar hopping handing out flyers that showed where Congress took 'charity' out of the Tax Code. In its place they put regulations for foundations...those who get money from one person and give it to another where charity had been defined as serving those in need with or without financial excess or salary. Volunteers gave their time once upon a time...they didn't get paid. I had looked in the Yellow Pages of my Phone Book and found the category no longer existed...so I researched it further. That event has come to be my reminder of what year America quit recognizing 'charity' as a worthwhile investment of time...even in the Tax Code it had never been about money...that is why a law governing the money cannot replace it... You should know this. Why?? Because the Tax Code reflects the behavior of America...or is that the other way around? Hey...THAT makes sense of Congress giving itself lifetime pension! Right? How can they hold a job after they prove they can't get along with coworkers and they aren't good decision makers and they certainly can't depend on charity...they outlawed it! Out-lawed...to make outside the Law...right? That's what happened to a lot of jobs you know...

Before I could finish the writing of this I received a Final Notice Bill from our electric company who by unprecedented grace is working with us this time only their unwavering terms state that if we split the bill like we split our rent payment and give them every penny over the rent of both unemployment checks this month we may keep our lights. That would mean a month and a half without running water...don't know yet what we will do...

My son's wedding is in days...word is people will put us in a motel room so we can clean up and stay instead of having to drive us back and forth. No one has money for our water bill and we need a house sitter as we have a dog who won't be attending the wedding. Only problem is the bath tub we had filled for flushing toilets runs out two days before we leave...now what? You can't stop pooping! Got a sitter in mind I might barter with but will he do survivalism 101 while we are gone? I don't know...this is what I call 'now what?'...

Baby Wipes and hand sanitizer are mandatory and paper products like paper towels and toilet paper and Styrofoam plates, cups and plastic silverware all make an amazing difference when the water is off as does candles and batteries when the lights are out. Consider this the 'poverty gift list' should you care to actually help someone in the same boat I'm in...show up with instant coffee and sugar or Instant Breakfast and Powdered Milk and you might get kissed! The offer of a shower or hot meal can be life changing... I had a neighbor who's phone I borrowed once to call my daughter...she caught on and without a word would just show up after having a bbq with a plate for us...just burgers and dogs but timing is everything and lonely hungry holidays expressly hard...her timing was always good! We have church group that has shown up with a bag of bread. There's a place about 9 blocks away that feeds bags of food to the homeless and if you go they will give you a bag...my husband can walk there and has a few times. Couple of times a year one group will help with utilities and another with real groceries every couple of months. We have had to go to them all before the food stamps came in and they don't make it no matter how hard we try...people make the difference...people who know how to help when it's needed without getting patted on the back or awarded at a big dinner...you don't need a charity name or tax deduction to be human... I have fed a man by the post office and a lady by the pawn shop on my better days in between hard times...you don't have to be rich just observant and willing...

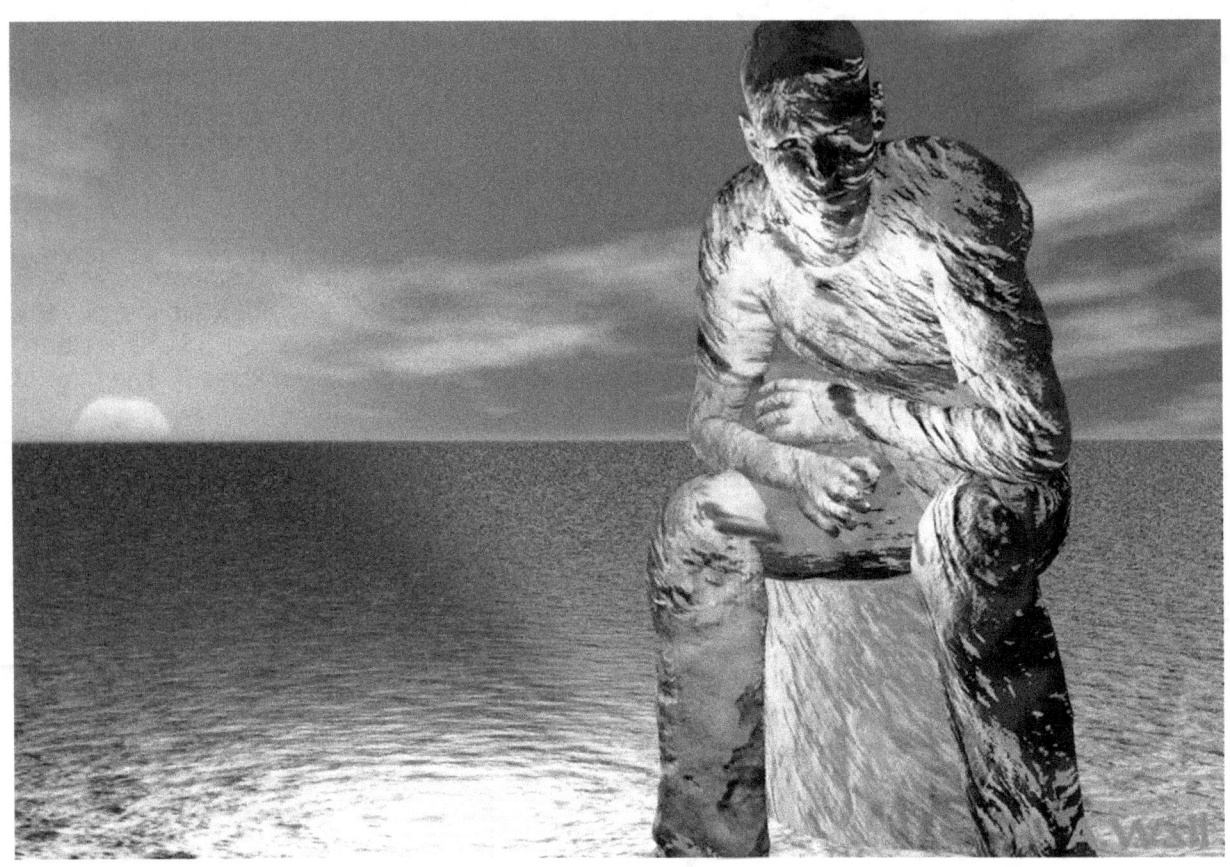

CHAPTER FIVE

Americans are learning what Europe learned after the World Wars...we are becoming European! People like me who had to do with little adopted new habits of conservation of things. My friend from Vienna told me how best to dry out plastic bags for reuse and how to polish and store my shoes and how to keep sweaters for years of wear. She knew where the local Shoe Repairs Store and Tailor were to prolong the use of what she wore. She was a Doctor and a pro at darning socks. In her closet she kept sealed dry foods just in case and explained why buying jewelry was always good because you could barter with it when there was no money. These were her values hard learned because of war. My friend who was married to the Ambassador to Russia for a time spoke of America product bottles kept for reuse there. The traditional recipes of England reflect times of wealth and no wealth with the standing idea that one could always make tea no matter what.

As I find myself shifting my personal habits to wrap around the idea that we are in a recession and I am a starving artist, I find these lessons haunt me as more practical than ever. I usually use one bowl and cup and limited silverware that I wash after using in case the water goes off...now I have a dish washer but I can't afford dish washing soap as often as one should and the electricity and water use make it prohibitive. I have gotten used to jugs of water always sitting in my bathroom full just in case. You wear the same clothes longer than normal when you can't afford regular laundry. You learn to use different corners of a hand towel to prolong its use too. You turn on the faucet before you sit on the pot to see if you get to flush it. You always fill your coffee maker before you go to bed just in case they come early to turn off the water. You tear paper towels in half to make them last longer. You give up going anywhere unless you have to. You overfill trash bags...anything that doesn't come on food stamps you conserve and it becomes habit. Food stamps pay roughly $3 a day a person and you find ways to make that work. My garden is the equivalent of the Victory Gardens planted at war's end but expressly more useful with tainted grocery concerns too. If you aren't doing these things you might consider it...because the twist comes at the end when it becomes the social norm and those who don't are looked down upon for their wasteful extravagance and it's coming like it did in Europe where they consider Americans wasteful!

Ben Franklin said neither a borrower nor lender be...somewhere he MUST be rolling over in his grave! (Not to mention his notion of free education...I keep recalling Lincoln walking 2 miles to borrow a book he read by candle light... and what that has become!) We are at a crossroads financially...banks and colleges became concerned when the internet was invented because they weren't sure their industries would continue to exist at all...rocked both industries to their roots! The end result of all this poor economy is the guy who has to pay cash because his credit has been ruined by events beyond his control but that won't go over well with criminology and even international sanction concepts because cash simply isn't necessarily written down as much making it much harder to trace. A crossroads...where we are going will shift...it has to. Paper trails are necessary...aren't they? How can you destroy 4 million people's credit (unemployment numbers from about 2 months ago) and maintain credit offering establishments and a stock market? Oh you can try to sing that song and dance but both are now beyond the wildest dreams of many. More than that...how can you fill jobs that require good credit scores? How can you possibly sell houses without credit? The sheer numbers are creating a financial tipping point. The federal government has discovered the value of giving poor people money on traceable cards for this reason but it will affect the rest of the financial community too. How many homeless people have no paper trails in America and are not on traceable unemployment and food stamps? Hey, they are Americans and many vote too! We, my husband and I, have been thrown into cash or nothing status and could not get a loan for anything. You establish credit and expenses based on income and when it suddenly disappears...you break your word like it or not. Can this be considered a judge of character? These are questions that will be answered and the tipping point is coming...what will come next I don't know. But I do know that phrases like a man is as good as his word and you can't get blood from a turnip and even the notion of debtors prison being reinstated come to mind when I ponder these things...something has to give on the big scale! There are just too many people like me...

My mother said to my shortly before she died at the ripe age of 76 when I told her about the beginnings of the internet that came to be after her death and how world wide I anticipated computer use to become that I had read too much science fiction. I have no fear of where we are going only hoping to survive to enjoy it! Today on the news they showed me a working model of Happy Potter's Invisibility Cloak...cool stuff is coming!

Wealthy people say poor people waste their money because they buy extravagant things when they get money. Poor people look at what wealthy people call normal and say the same thing. It's a feast a famine thing really...you have nothing and wish for something then you get the opportunity and having seen opportunities snatched away before you try to acquire the things you have sat around wanting for so long, when you have the chance you act quickly. Then you have what I like to call the Pie-Hole Problem. You only get one Pie-Hole...someone gives you five bucks...if you are me since that amount won't save the world my first thought is a good cup of coffee only I always settle for a good brew at a gas station for about $2...I have been to Star Bucks once I think. But then I have to have my nicotine...I buy $1 cigars and feel like I did something since I don't have to smoke left over tobacco in my pipe. Sweets and sometime protein is the next thought because they are hard to come by...that's three things...I only have one Pie-Hole thus the Pie-Hole Problem. If you are really hungry and nicking out and dying for that cup of coffee there is NO right order to consume them...and you cannot consume them all at the same time no matter how bad you want to! I know...I have tried...its the Pie-Hole Problem!

My daughter didn't make it to my house yesterday as planned...my water is still on and I don't know why...and today I got sugar and coffee! Whoo-hoo! I mention this because everything you value comes into play every day in my situation...like doing what you said you would. Should you be upset after hurting because I had to wait a day for coffee and sugar after a week of no sugar and instant and the paper towels are running out for the bathroom! It is a value lesson! My daughter doesn't have to come at all you know...I am lucky! Turns out an anxious bride to be got to my daughter first. My son gets married this month and my attendance 4 hours away falls heir to whoever can get me there and what I will wear was purchased for me. Unfortunately there was a transportation disconnect between my daughter's house and mine until she rescued me from no lights. See I live in an adult environment and smoke in my house so the bride trying to make everything perfect and being a non-smoker herself wanted the dress for me stored at my daughter's house so it doesn't smell smokey which is understandable. I didn't get to try it on until my lights went off. It didn't fit...my daughter took it to a tailor yesterday instead of coming to see me... Now there is nothing I can do about any of the decisions made in my behalf...fortunately I have a phone this time so I know why she didn't come unlike other times when I just sat and waited until I became scared for her well being and met her with tears when she did show...I want to go to my son's wedding! What to think? You learn to accept such things and just go on...eventually you begin to talk yourself into wanting less and expecting less and less of people so you don't get disappointed so often. First you go through a stage of feeling less important than the entire universe to the people you love most and everything they want for themselves seems superfluvious and ostentatious while you go without ...you reassess everything. They don't know what to do with your situation either...first they blame you for it too! Especially when you raise your kids to see a problem and solve it but there is no solution this time and I did...they are excellent problem solvers every one of them!   I had a friend who was an actress turned fashion designer who quit wearing jewelry because her jewelry was stolen...I have had all my jewelry stolen 3 times in my life and I still wear jewelry but I think of her because I have given up lots of things I used to call normal because it only hurts your feelings when they are taken away...great expectations cause greater loss. My daughter says she is coming today...I am hopeful! I still don't know why my water is on... Me? I hope...I love...and I am grateful for any help I get but it took time to get here...

My daughter's new husband has landed a terrific job 4 hours away from me...she won't be coming to my rescue once she moves (she should have already moved)...I am just glad to see her smile... I am convinced this is where high tea comes from...getting to see someone smile and making the visit last longer by serving more goodies... Celebrate the common things, you know? Like hugging the runaway child once found...it doesn't make sense but it's real...

My child is NOT supposed to be rescuing me at all! I am so glad she does... This is absurd!

You don't have to believe in something to appreciate it. I once interviewed a one-eyed homeless vet on camera for a show that never came to fruition we called The Point attempting to bring reality to the common guy that didn't know why people were on the streets. He explained to me that he had stolen food and slept in the doorway of a church that had the most gruesome gargoyles I've ever seen over the doorways just to be safe. He said you do what you have to like I should understand that...he repeated it several times to be clear. I still don't understand crime like that because I would like to think I wouldn't do it. I never have. In one of my incarnations I was a very good Security Guard but that job won't be mine again as you have to physically able to make something safe. This morning I went when the store opened next to my house to get my coffee but the clerk had to go get sugar in the back. A delivery guy watched me while she did this and I know that look...perhaps he was looking because I walk with a stick...arthritis...martial arts...you choose but it makes you feel like a lesser person to be looked at like you might steal something. He didn't know me or my history so he was right to look! I guess stealing food is more common than I know...its never crossed my mind to take advantage of people to get ahead like criminals think...I waited, got my stuff and came home...

Is your first thought when you run to the bathroom, 'oh god please let it work'? That's right I can turn on the light this time and oh good there's toilet paper because my daughter came by... Poverty creeps into the psyche uninvited... My daughter did make it by yesterday and there was this awkward discussion outside my front door as we were trying to leave for the store...see dehydration had led me to the stupid desire to drink lots of coffee and rehydrate which I did only to find myself nearly faint by the time she got here because I hadn't slept. Her feet hurt...I didn't look like someone she wanted to shop with...my husband is faster in a store and she had to get home to the kids...her cigarettes were in the car and I really wanted the additives not in cheap cigars so I really wanted one...I was trying! Took a step and had to grab the wall behind me as I almost swooned...love that word as its old south...but anyway went light headed for a moment and decided the store was too much as it turns out sitting too much and reusing tobacco from tobacco butts in a pipe has the effect of creating excess phlegm almost to the point of pneumonia and it can slow you right down! Anyway...husband decided he would go and had to dress because even he saves his dress clothes because of laundry issues...I decided to go sit down so I told her sore feet and all to please just get me a proper smoke before she goes and I laid down while my husband...poor man...tried to recall all I thought we would need not knowing when she would come again and we would have access to a grocery store knowing all the while he would forget something and I would remember it. Poor man...he tries so hard! She brought me smokes...they leave. Then come the tears and the texts...I am soooo sorry! Meant to be ready! My fault! Oh god that disapproving look on your face when you looked me over...I am sooo sorry I didn't dress right too (she hates me in sweats and a sweater and I didn't get my hair brushed just pulled it back...gonna lose the long hair...I know it!) Anyway...things were gotten...half the money is gone and we might make it three days without another store visit. See, the convenient store is too expensive but sometimes all we have we can get to because car insurance is too expensive so we can't drive our otherwise legal vehicle out front and we only get $3 per person per day so one has to carefully plan every penny and I just didn't get that far this time because I am writing instead silly me! Anyway, its all too hard to figure out without inside knowledge and a plan...a neighbor walked by as this was going on and who knows what they thought they saw... All hard feelings just thrown away...my girl comes back with the great white hunter and his catch of the day within the hour. I muttered explanations to her and she tells my husband to make me push fluids...there is toilet paper and cigars now. He makes me a cup of coffee...I am so lucky! She calculates her life and figures when she might come back...the tailor couldn't fit the dress...too little fabric...she shows me a picture on her phone of what look like silver bedroom slippers and tells me these are my shoes for the wedding and I thank her (only one ex at this wedding and I don't care to impress him anyway...I could say that with a smile even if I would never have owned those shoes of my own volition). Then we joke about where my corset is to squeeze me into the dress because there are no choices and only ten days to go. My daughter mutters something about when she will leave for the wedding and says something about we will have to just figure my ride out...whatever that means. I do hope I get to go! I'll wear whatever they like...I have been promised one dance before my son moves to Massachusetts...I want my dance! I produced him a piece of art to hang on his wall in Boston so he won't forget me...I can't afford to buy a print. I produced the art for T-Shirt and made them available on Zazzle for the Girl's Night out, the Stag Party, an ornament for their first married Christmas that I will likely miss...even a mug for his Bachelor Party...can't buy them myself and no one else has but I contributed! I want my dance. I hope I get to go. My daughter will come again in five days and I will be ready this time.

I wonder if my writing style will be accepted. I could work on best grammar and wording but my intention is to show an outpouring of self so I am writing as I think...bits and pieces...raw emotion in simple terms. Mine isn't a story made for movie and I can write such too. This isn't fine poetry with careful timber and alliteration and I can write that too. My son to be married in ten days has a college degree in English and his bride does too working in the field of technical writing...neither will approve of this. This is my life and I am sharing it because my daughter thought someone might be interested enough to buy it and I want to make a living so I can change my life...what a cycle!

Ah ha! I have to poop! Been waiting three days now! Hydrated enough that my body is beginning to work normally...now to build my strength walking more! Did my breathing exercises and mostly cleared my lungs...getting better all the time...ten days to get to dance...there has to be a way! They want me to not use my walking stick and look normal...that they may have to live with but if there is a way...I will get there...I will dance! Feed me wine and relieve my pain and I can forget all this...then I surely can dance...danced with my daughter at her wedding and surprised everyone...I want to dance again!

This is the war after the war...we are more European all the time...

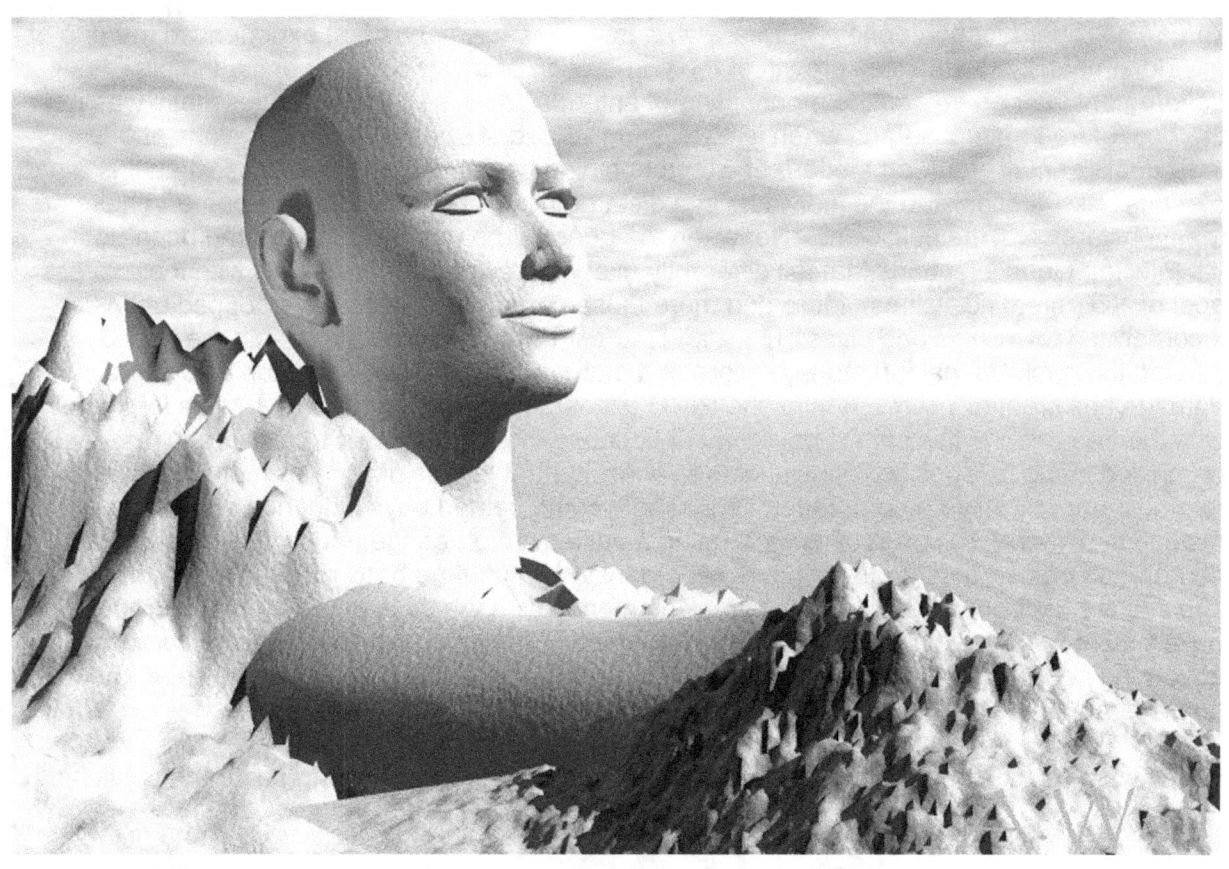

~ CHAPTER SIX ~

Democracy at it's finest is supposed to be like Japanese Pilinko Game and not like Sudoku. You have a set number of possible end holes and you pour in the ball bearing and see where they go and what configuration plays out every time you play... First there is the Capital in Washington where the Ball Bearings go in then they trickle down to the states to alter meaning of specifics of legislation then down to the Counties then Cities and towns then the Ball Bearings get hauled back up to the Capital through the Judicial system according to how they fell and a new batch is readied to dump. On the other hand Corporate America is like Sudoku...only so many numbers can fit in each square and no matter how original each square...the rows and columns are limited to the same answers over and over again giving the impression of randomization but with a specific set limit to possibilities over all. Real randomness lives in the Pilinko Game and in the human heart. Over time you come to realize that its 1 through 9 no matter how you look at it in Sudoku but the number of balls that fall and which holes they may fill can never be predicted. The analogy comes to my mind because of an experiment run in the early 90's at Princeton using a Pilniko game and postulating whether people could influence the fall of the balls...that's a reflection of politics isn't it? Either a person can or can't influence the fall of the balls...look how few people influence decisions made by corporations? Sudoku...the goal remains the same old boring goal of making money no matter how you place the numbers. See its people making gain with no regard for others we call monsters. Be it criminals, governments, murderers and thieves or armies and corporations...or especially Vampires and Werewolves in scary urban mythology. The equation is always the same...no regard for someone. There are always victims. America first experienced the grip of this during early industrialized growth of the corporation and its subtle fingers in the pie of our government later on mandating monopoly and anti-trust laws...cut throat ruthlessness was not the goal of free enterprise and when it rears its ugly head, it speaks to the decisions of the individual or small group on a board of directors hiding behind corporate shields when it is a part of a business, it speaks to the individual in a dictatorship or the individual in a crime. Those are the monsters! Not the politicians. Not when the good of the people is the agreed upon goal. It's Pilinko! Good intentions that fall differently every time we swap politicians with the express goal of NOT creating victims. More and more those corporate shields have popped up in incorporated townships and cities. More and more it becomes tempting to shift the goal of serving the public to making money. More and more ruthlessness in acceptable collateral damage has created victims. I think the RICO act established in the 80's has had a lot to do with the free reign of this shift in government because the stipulation in that law requires organized crime for specific financial gain to enact it...that leaves out government officials turning democracy into a corporation where the income gained buys influence and power instead of a yacht. By virtue of it never being modified it creates the appearance that a corporation or incorporated township is not organized crime if no body gains money from it. Oh salaries are ok though. Oh the goal of making money as a whole is ok shifting the purpose of government from serving the public to making money. Why would anyone want a corporate governing body? That turns townships into shell companies! They don't want to serve the public at all! Sudoku doesn't work...Democracy does...

I don't want my government to make money like a corporation...I want it to serve the public at large!

I am the birth of the American Economic Refuge...and a starving artist! I am incredibly patriotic but I think I am a throw back from the original version of the documents. The Judicial system is the defining body of those documents as intended and not street politics. Congress works (when it works) to write bills for the greater good of our nation and not with short foresight to benefit small groups. The words should be lofty and broad not narrow and specialized...we the people did not list every small segment of the American humanity by virtue of a category yet laws were written to include them all. We may be acting like a fractured mind on the large scale but by state there are also no lofty words to serve us all in written law. You know...like people should be individually responsible and held liable for damages incurred during a wreck because it is the right thing to do so say we all and its for the good of all the people that you do instead of writing you will have this much insurance from this approved company or we will take your car and won't let you drive any vehicle legally because no one pays their debts and assumes responsibility when there is a wreck. See what I mean? Used to be there were people who did the right thing because it was the right thing and everyone knew who didn't! I mention the insurance companies not because of my issues with my car but because of their new function of information gathering. My situation will fully shift once it is realized that everyone without insurance on their car or their health aren't feeding data to the data gatherers...that's a given! But for the moment...medical care has shifted because of it...no not just the increased cost where one political party is trying to make the other one look bad but the actual info being gathered has altered treatment!. Some of this is good. I think the CDC should have particulars about the whole country they didn't have before and I am not concerned about data mining so much by private enterprises but I am concerned when health care becomes more about gathering this data and assuming diagnosis can be done in a formatted way. The Unified Theory of Physics was one thing...the Unified Code of Justice another but when going to the doctor constitutes a list of blood tests and the thin veil that somehow those numbers alone can diagnose you is quite another. If we had all the answers it would be different...that might work but we do not know if what works on one person CAN work on another...there can be no Unified Health Diagnosis Program. It just won't work. Health simply is not a metaverse project! Health care by statistic??? Come on...that's just a bad joke!

Before I leave the topic of Patriotism I want to say what I never say out loud because of the ongoing war between parties and how you get beat up for choosing a side even on the small scale locally in everyday life and you do. I have had enough body blows to no longer want to enter the fray even verbally. I am third generation Democrat of the John Kennedy variety...a firm believer in the statement, 'ask not what your country can do for you but ask yourself...what can _you_ do for your country'. I have to say that clearly to continue because it dictates many of my behaviors. I have friends who say why don't you get on disability...surely you are damaged enough to get it but I won't try. I would rather risk my well being this way than 'cost' my country any more than I have to. I didn't want food stamps...my husband kind of snuck that in on me and he had good reason. Of course I am glad we have good food but actually go get them? I never would have on my own. I would and have to a great extent found another way some of which I am writing about here. I believe in the free enterprise form of government...I want to work for a living. I don't like the idea that we are living on unemployment no matter how many people tell me like the commercial to get settlement payments in a lump sum, 'it's your money...have it when you want it!'. No matter how many times I hear the idea that the government is your mother...I never took advantage of her either though some thought I did. This Democrat does not believe in a socialized America no matter how many times you hear it said by those not Democrats so remember you read this...not ALL Democrats believe in a socialized America and I think we are penalized for it. I believe in my government _more_ since 911 only because I would not have the tactic expressed as the sole purpose for terrorism in the book the Art of War succeed...it is used to turn people against their authority and when I watch the news I worry because a lot of people on the public stage do not sound like me. Surely I am not the only one who has read the Art of War...Schwartzkoff had it on his book stand during Desert Storm. Surely the spirit of Americans after 911 still rings true and there is a market for this book among people trying to ride out a storm like me right here. I have to believe that. I have been damaged by life and I have to find a way to survive without becoming a burden of the state. That's what this book is really all about to me. I would not embarrass myself telling my story if pity was what it inspired...if anger at someone else was born from my difficulties. This book is tips and how to's for those fighting the fight to survive in a damaged America like me. John Kennedy also said. 'young men have visions and old men dream dreams'...I might argue that one as I'm not so young anymore and I have a vision of America that says this is a transition period from the things we have tried that didn't work to a closer form of the original written democracy that reminds people of the human value of people. We can all become statistics and bytes in a mega verse but we cannot become less human doing it. I can see it...it can work! In the future I envision people helping people large scale not in petty little groups who shout the loudest. I don't like doing things the hard way but my spirit is not broken nor will it be as long as America stands because as long as she stands there is hope for me finding my way to work for a living in a way I can continue because I will keep trying to do that as long as I breathe...

I plan to stay here a long time! My mother used to joke that old age wasn't so bad if you consider the alternative. It would appear that reduced caloric intake increases life span! Surprise...I couldn't have begged myself to go without this much on purpose and it appears it may promote longevity in me! That said...I am also a lifelong martial artist. In the 80's books began to be translated and made available in the U.S. from China. Things changed after Bruce Lee had his back broken for spilling secrets and Nixon open relations with China. They have a totally different point of view about survival than you will find at your local fitness center. In about 600BC (I'm guessing at the year but most Taoist Practices go back that far) Da Mo sat in front of a wall for years at a Shaolin Monastery...when he got up he wrote Eight Pieces of Brocade which is an exercise set to save the lives of monks who were dying seeking enlightenment in sedentary ways. It is an excellent read if you are interested. Tells you how to sit all the time and do these simple things for circulation and flexibility and to benefit your organs so you can stay alive while you thus damage you body by sitting too much. I only mention that book here because people don't know about it not because I am expert enough to teach it. That's one useful tool in my survival arsenal and Fragrant Chi Gung is yet another. The introduction to the story of Da Mo included that his age was never known as it was possible that he changed identities many times and lived many lives before his actual death but that most considered he lived to about 200. Believe it or not and I am writing from memory so that isn't exact but as I recall it. Today you can find both online for practicing or just for curiosity. Remarkably one of the healing tools used by Chinese artists in rural areas are drawings...it is their form of psychology. They consider that if your head is on wrong you need to see a different view and they make drawing by means I do not know and give them like a prescription to their patients with orders to meditate on them so much for so long like a pill prescription here. I find that fascinating being an artist! Now that is art...I can only hope some piece I do will move someone and that falls to the realm of the medical profession there. There are also rumors of Arians...monks who appear to live on air alone. There is a mountain where a Taoist monk used to live and they say he lived on a weed that grew near his cave and he meditated sitting on a tree that extends straight out from the mountain over 3000 feet above sea level (got a picture of that!) but the $10,000 reward is for anyone who can read what he wrote above his cave because no one can figure out how he got up there to write it! I mention these things to rattle your cage about what can and cannot be done. In the oldest documents of Traditional Chinese Medicine you find early Taoist Practices. I have studied what I could find. It needs to be tried and considered as simply what works...I don't even think science know why this stuff works or what tongue diagnosis is about at all. I will not say I understand these things I am about to explain to the best of my grasp of things beyond me...they work. I am still here...not sure I would be if they didn't work...I am lucky to know these things...

I have to say the predominate force in staying alive is the will to live. These exercises have to be done to work. If I were you I would question your will to live if you find no value here...I do not do these exercises because I want to exercise or impress people with weird ancient oriental knowledge or because I understand the real difference they make and I wonder about that every time I do them! I do them because they are supposed to help you stay well and live longer and those things I want to do...when I put off doing these exercises when I know I need to do them I wonder about my will to survive...it's that simple...I am still here...these things help.

First let me send you where you can get a better education than the one I offer her about Taoism. Http://www.UniversalTao.com...anything written by Master Mantak Chia...he has a place in Thailand. I should also mention out of respect that David Carradine who was a lifelong martial artist and even practiced with Bruce Lee who also believed everyone had the right to know how best to survive. David Carradine knew this stuff even producing Chi Gung video tapes for people to learn from and my all time favorite martial arts movie entitled Circle of Iron as his tribute to Bruce Lee. I do not believe David Carradine committed suicide but there was a fatal mistake made. Chuck Norris is in his 70's...he knows a few things too...Stephen Segal knows a whole bunch more...je paid his dues!

I intend to tell my understanding of Taoist Practice as it is in my head to show you that full understanding is not necessary. This book is not a research piece though I have much more information on my book shelves and could go there. What is in my head is what I use and what works for me...it's not all but enough. It should therefore be enough for you too...

There is an exercise that comes to mind when my lungs feel heavy. I check my breathing all the time...I smoke! Usually I have found 2 things that keep me from breathing deeply though my western doctor suggested emphazema or possibly COPD but my lungs contract and expand just fine when there isn't major gas under my ribs or congestion in them or something is dislocation that won't allow my ribs to raise when I breathe air in. There are Taoist exercises that get rid of both. Breathing is everything! Don't you agree?

I believe the gas fixing exercise may have something to do with that valve I mentioned before because that's how I learned about it...it's the placement of hands that got me curious and when I looked it up I found the valve is right where you press. You sit straight in a chair knees fairly close together and sit straight. Put your hands in front of you over your knees with your palms facing inward say towards your face. You have to look at your palms. That's important they say to establish an eye hand connection. Not sure why that is important but it doesn't work if you don't do it. With finger tips touching you raise your arms up to eye level breathing in deeply through your nose then you pivot your hands so they are point inward and push them into you abdomen about half way between your belly button and your hip on your left side. Push in fairly deeply and breathe out through your mouth making the sound 'who' and hold it leaning into your hands slightly. Think of your spleen and your pancreas colored yellow. Think of the season Indian Summer when the world feels like it is standing still in the seasonal wheel almost like the top of a leap in dance class...that pregnant pause of a season before fall. Recall a moment when you felt the pause in a natural environment and try to feel that feeling again just for a moment. Realize you are a part of the world and the natural environment as well. Then return your hands to your lap and consider where you just went and what it felt like and like you hug a child imagine hugging your yellow pancreas and spleen with love. You will burp. Your belly will quit producing gas. What is there will disappear one way or another...you'll feel better! Then you will breathe better!

I have read some medical research referring to gas under the left ribs near the pancreas as being common in x-ray before heart attacks...I have read that Pancreatitis feels like a knife through your body at the same point but I can tell you that the T-11 being dislocated can also cause that feeling and some difficulty controlling your diaphragm which effects breathing also but this exercise always helps me and I'll get to aligning your back later. It's hard to fill your lungs when everything under your diaphragm is pushing to occupy the same space...poop or air! Lack of oxygen to the brain makes you ditsy...you must have a clear head when under the duress of poverty. Try the exercise...it costs nothing and the only thing stopping you now is you...

The sounds produced best I can tell are a remarkable concept in themselves. There actually is a martial art of sounds but its really hard to locate. I found myself wanting to know about them after practicing Taoist exercises and recognizing a comparison to something remarkable I saw in formal class once. I had dislocated both hips and my master had put them back in place for me. I then couldn't free spar for awhile so I did basic movements and katas for 2 and a half hours. You can exhaust yourself doing katas if you work towards perfection and it seemed reasonable that I was given an opportunity and should then do that. Worn out at the end of class the master called the few of us doing this over to show him what we had learned. I put everything into my attempt because it was afterall for the master! He just said do it again. So we all did somewhat considerable with less energy than before. He said do it again. Hoping to move through it at all he then Kiaed (is that a word?) The sound that came out of him came from the bottom of his belly...it was unusual enough to be noted. I had more energy...in fact I felt fresh like I was just starting out! I looked at him with my best puzzled look and when I finished he called me too him and pulled out a black marker and wrote Korean symbols on the left side of my ToBok. People told me that was my name...I never found out...2 house fires and 17 burglaries later my ToBok was just gone and I don't even know what happened to it! Something about that sound changed me...of that I was certain. (They just turned my water off! Oh my...I can't wash my hands or flush my toilet with running water any more! Maybe next week that luxury will be mine again...they won't give us an extension again for like six months now because we got an extension and didn't pay like we said we would before we borrowed the money for the lights and had to pay it back...that's not good.) Ok...so I have seen there is a name for the martial study of sound but I can't recall it just now nor could I afford the books to teach me those things but they are out there if you are interested. What I can tell you is it is said when you do these exercises and make the appropriate sound you should vibrate it to the point you are meditating on. Logic says that can't be done. Remarkably I can tell you that you punch from the bottom of your feet and logically that can't be done either but I know it can be done. In the case of the punch its a matter of actually having a kind of control over every molecule you possess and it comes after much practice. Trained reflexes are afterall trained muscle memory. I saw what I saw and felt what I felt so I have to believe it...right? I can tell you Taoist sounds over time do reverberate at least through your chest...didn't to begin with but over time it starts to and the more regularly you do them the deeper that sound can be felt into your body. I can tell you Tai Chi masters say the same thing. I can tell you, you use different throat muscles for each sound and it pulls on different pieces of you to use the different sets of muscles. I can also tell you that in itself could be healing by understanding of acupuncture pressure points and their function. I think of it like a stringed instrument when muscle vibrates and that vibrates tendons...the sounds may seem silly but someone somewhere thought this whole thing through...that's why people are called masters... I am not a master and only a fair practitioner...

The Lung exercise comes next...like the turn of the seasons...it is Fall which follows Indian Summer. Sitting in the same position with your hands in the same starting position...look at your palms and keeping your eyes there raise your hands over your head breathing in through your nose. Once you are looking straight up and your lungs are full (How full is full? Stretch them!). Flip your palms to the ceiling and breathe out making the sound 'hsss' while using your stomach muscles to empty your lungs...start by tightening them just above the pubic bone and tightening them all the way up. (If your first thought is you can't do this, the right thought is you don't know how and you cannot learn how unless you try...muscle memory right? Over time your brain will learn to actually control your body better! What you have just learned is that there are pieces of you you forget all the time...and you think you feel like you are alive...) Feel the lungs emptying and think of the element metal and the colors lavender and gray. Imagine the first crisp air of fall and a moment in time when it tasted like champagne to you...crisp and life giving! (Gimme more!) Like the dance, the Limbo, how empty can you go? Feel the diaphragm pushing upward too? It should do that with every breath you breathe...but you ignore it. In the movie Remo Williams they joke about learning to breath but you have to be taught to pay attention to yourself breathing to actually know when something isn't working right. Breathing air takes in oxygen and exhales impurities...your animal brain parts do this without you controlling it so its easy to ignore but it feels really good to breathe if you pay attention and sounds reverberate through the air environment your lungs provide. Feel that! How you breathe can tell you how you feel in everyday life. Shallow rapid breathing is common to fear...you may think things don't scare you but when you pay attention to your breathing you find you are breathing like they do! You may surprise yourself! Anyway, at the emptying of your lungs lower your arms and think about hugging your lungs just like you hugged your spleen with love. You will find when you think about it you have real emotion because anyone not really grateful their organs work is just nuts! If you really would survive your gratitude is absolutely sincere...

There are five such exercises in all. They begin the same way...the breathing is the same...the organ, sound, season, element, and exhaling posture differ.

Winter is the Kidneys and their color is Blue...the exhaling posture is leaning forward over your knees. You will come to see since the Kidneys are at the base of your rib cage to your back that the exhaling posture applies discrete pressure on each organ you would consider. Winter is the contracting of the world like ice freezing and its cold! Think your Kidneys cold and contracting and recall a moment in with when the world felt like that and try to refeel that feeling! They say the human body is 90 something percent water and it all goes through your Kidneys! Boy are they important! Don't you just love them for keeping you alive? In Tai Chi they say the Kidneys produce the Jing which is where Chi comes from...I have seen a scientific explanation by a Taoist engineer of some credentials explain the electricity connection. Water keeps you alive. The military postulate I call the Law of Threes says you can survive 3 minutes without air, 3 days without water and 30 days without food...never tried this in extreme but I would believe the military. Heck...I would believe a Tai Chi Master! I live doing Shiatzu...they say it was born of the natural urge to touch where it hurts! I have found knowing a few points and knowing what it feels like to drain one that needs it...oooie!! Points can even produce a skin effect when it needs to be messed with! First the muscle will knot usually though but if you feel for the point and apply constant pressure and don't chicken out because the right point needing work always hurts like hell when you find it until it doesn't...I have to believe in the stuff. My mother came to believe in it when she was having terrible leg cramps. In a hospital setting I have had her actually make a doctor, a nurse and her friend who was a chiropractor stand back to let me stop her leg cramps...I have a knack for Shiatzu. The sound for the Kidneys is, 'wooo' like the would 'woe'...now if while reading this and doing nothing more you make that sound and pay attention to the muscles you use you will find your solar plexus tightening which from the inside of you punches on the Kidneys...lean over and it does it better! This is me sneaking in on you the very idea of 'how' to look at these exercises. It is not what you know they do...it is what you learn by doing them...eventually when your body clues you to something that needs to be touched you learn your own little ways to do those things. No gym required...might look like a stretch in an office instead. The man who taught me says he does the Kidney exercise while driving because he tires and his Kidneys ache driving! It becomes a way of life and not some fancy something to show your friends...this is the truth of martial artistry...it is the art of survival...

Liver is the Spring...little plants pushing up from the still cold ground looking to grow. The color is Green. The exhale posture is like the Lungs but lean to the right with your hands over your head which applies physical pressure on the Liver that lives under your left rib cage to the front of you. Did I forget to mention entwining your fingers? You should do that when you move your hands from your knees to begin the exercises always. The entwined fingers actually reflects Muhdra but that's another story and it's based partly on pressure points but more on the function of conditioning. Muhdra is the art of finger posturing used in meditation. The Muhdra that relates to naturally entwined fingers is the old Church with a steeple hand posture that everybody knows from childhood and has done. See in the orient hand postures are a science and they are related to behaviors. The Muhdra is the fingers entwined on the inside of your hands with the pointers touching...I am suggesting you entwine your fingers on the outside when raising your hands over your head in the Taoist exercise not connecting the pointer fingers separately...a more passive hand posture. Now its called a micro expression or body language function (or a tell in lie detecting and poker!) when say a lecturer makes a steeple usually with the fingers on the outside and the pointers connecting and it infers holding a body of knowledge and imparting it piece by piece which is why you will likely see a lecturer do this hand posture. It's perfectly natural and normal to do so without cognitive thought. The Muhdra of entwining to the inside of your hands is unusual...it is meant to be. It can be used as a language like sign language or just for the purpose of meditation and it has a specific meaning. The idea is that you find the true meaning within yourself though you can find loads of translations for Muhdra published. The reason a master will teach Muhdra is that what a student will find within themselves when they practice a specific Muhdra should match what the master found when developing the body of study because if well trained he put that understanding within his student. So a Muhdra can literally be used as a test. The Muhdra of a fist under an open hand that everyone who has ever seen a formal martial arts class in a movie or even the formal fighting posture before the bow has a specific meaning...hidden knowledge or it is sometimes said hidden power which is where the phrase knowledge is power actually comes from. So whether you give a specific meaning to your hand postures or look for meaning in them within yourself or signal a stranger that you have hidden knowledge...when you entwine your fingers I want you to think of Taoist exercises and your will to survive all the extraordinary crazy times we are living in! The wringing of hands...a form of entwining fingers is the common hands posture for not knowing what to do...now you know! Check yourself and see which exercise would benefit you most at this moment! What is a survivor's guide if it doesn't help you survive? This is how conditioning works...this is how you train your subconscious with arts that can save you from dying...this is the whole purpose of being a martial artist. Does it work? Will you now notice hands? You decide... The Liver sound is 'shhh" like you are hushing a baby...

I can't flush my toilet like you normally do and wash my hands without juggling a jug! What a freaking drag! I have to uncondition the normal behavior of flushing to not flushing like when the lights go out and my husband and I laugh at ourselves and at how many light switches we flip that serve no purpose at all! I just had to mention that since this book is about the art of survival. How long do you have to do something before it becomes habit? They say fifteen days. Oh good...not flushing normally for only five days shouldn't screw me up too badly then as I really want to remain acceptable among the normal people who flush every time! We have been through this stuff so many times in 18 months that it causes a hesitation...turn the light on or off? Flush after using the bathroom? It screws with your brain in subtle ways. Homeless people open packs of cigarettes from the bottom because they might give a cigarette away and they don't know where the hands reaching for a cigarette (or their own) have been so it is more sanitary! It's all subtle conditioning...then someone looks at the guy on a street corner and wonders why they seem like a different species of people almost...the stuff changes people. I met the clever girl at a day labor job I had once who taught me the cigarette thing. She was smart because she always carried a two liter with Kool-Aid in it and a couple of straws so she could safely share...lol...Kool-Aid is cheaper than soda and she knew about dehydration especially digging ditches which we did that day and her straws did feel better than no straw when she kept me from passing out in the Florida sun because I wasn't so smart myself (ok...I couldn't even afford Kool-Aid that day...). At least I got to dig ditches! The day before I had come and they insisted I go and apply for a house keeping job at a hotel but with my credentials I was qualified for their Security Department and so there was no opening for me (they had so many questions...what...was I supposed to lie?) and thus no days pay and no dinner and no Kool-Aid! I looked too sophisticated to dig ditches they said. The world gets weird when you try to survive...people believe what they see and do not hear what you say...I told them I needed work that day...they told me I was better than a ditch digger...it was a hungry night and she was the smart one when I finally got to my ditch! I ate dinner that night and the next day brought my own Kool-Aid! Had an interesting conversation with the Horticulturist in charge of the landscaping project too! Had to be careful and look dumber than I was or he might not have let me come back and dig the next day too...screwed up somewhere and only got to work on my ditch for a couple of days but the office had caught on by then and let me do construction clean up next...I finally worked my way up to house keeping at a hotel that was a lot easier on my back and I ate all the way there! A friend got me a bath at a friend of his' house after a couple of days too...that was a long time ago but you never forget...at least I have a roof tonight and lights!

People believe what they want to believe. No truer words were ever said with the possible exception that people also do what they really want to do. People also make of you what they will and give authority to whomever they choose. I have had a lot of fun trying to consider the criteria people work from. You might think it comes from upbringing and it partly does and you might think it comes from chosen doctrine like religion and part of it does but I think it comes from somewhere else. Like why an artist is an artist. You will believe in these exercises or not and I have no idea what your reasons will be. I can tell you this...I haven't listed them so I can sit back and laugh at the stupid thing I have suggested you do. I told you my reason...what will be your response? I swear it's Plinko! The American way... Will you help me survive by learning what will help you survive? Isn't that an interesting question?

I just scared the lady blowing leaves off my patio! That thing is so noisy she didn't hear me open the patio door so I touched her shoulder to get her attention and she about jumped out of her skin! I didn't mean to scare her...just wanted to thank her for her hard work...people should thank people more often. I was impressed by Jackie O who is most remembered by her thank you notes. People remember being thanked. Last Security Course I took 2 years ago before I realized my body said no, the instructor made a deal of introducing me to the class and he used the words 'thank you for your service' which nearly threw me into tears! I have never been military and I save that phrase for the real public servants who know that's what they are...the military, police and fire guys. I was shocked! See I have been the director of a nonprofit organization in my crazy life that brought Christmas to literally thousands of children and he knew it. No one ever thanked me for that except him. Mostly people just thought I could survive anything because I could help them...period! It was a funny end result actually. You tell someone you have a problem hoping they will help you and people would honestly tell me they knew I would figure it out because of what they had seen me do...never hearing my plea for help! Life can be so strange...

The Heart Exercise I saved for last. It is the source of all compassion it is said. It's also the pump that keeps you on this plain of existence a little longer...but basically it's just a pump...right? Now I really don't know why the Heart exercise works but it does. Did I mention that when you make your sound you will notice different tastes and temperatures in your mouth? I think they seem diagnostic myself and perhaps they are related to the Chinese flavors used for medicinal food but if you have the flu and do the Lung exercise you will taste (I don't want to say this because I can see my daughter going...oh gross!) puss. when the infection is gone so is the flavor because the Lung exercise will make you cough and clear your lungs as it is supposed to in fact when sick I will do it until the lungs are clear enough to suit me and then daily until the bad taste goes away. Healthy Lungs produce a kind of metallic taste! When you do the Heart exercise and make the sound 'haaa' meditating on the color red and the season Summer imagining heat radiating from you like hot flesh on a warm day radiates heat you will feel heat in your mouth. Just wanted to mention that. You will learn your own lessons or laugh about how silly all this sounds to you like me kids have until it helps them... The exhale posture is hands over your head and leaning to the right where the heart resides. I find that I feel a sense of self pushing forth when I do that exercise...a trueness of me...or whatever you might call that and don't forget to hug your heart when you are done...it always reminds me of curling up in front of a fireplace with a snuggly blanket or like being hugged as a child. I think people love children like they love a pet animal with an open heart. Adults hug adults differently. A hug can lower high blood pressure and I have wondered if 'hugging your heart' in this manner does too but I haven't been able to test it with a blood pressure cuff yet though I have thought how crazy people would think me in the grocery store if I did the exercise and tested my blood pressure twice on the blood pressure devices there...before and after...just to find out. These exercises do throw off emotional angst of different sorts depending on the exercise. When I learned them I was taught to meditate on the emotion specific to the exercise and I have found that part doesn't matter as the effect occurs without it. Thus I have not listed them here. If you do these things you will have your own understanding of what they do and that is far more important than me explaining...I once told a Hindu friend of mine that I didn't have much faith in myself and he quickly said my heart was beating...what, did I think it would stop? When crying over a lost love at the age of 14 I decided you could not cry yourself to death...I have since learned of what is called a 'broken heart syndrome' that can actually cause a heart attack. I am glad I know this exercise. It has no doubt saved my life...

There is an Iron Shirt exercise that can straighten your back without a chiropractor and it's fairly straightforward and simple. Basically it uses the muscles of your own back to push the vertebrae into their normal postures. It seems to me that it also relaxes parts that tighten up holding your back out but that's what I think. Take 2 chairs...put them far enough apart that you can put your head on one and your heels on the other then do so. That's it! Now I have done all kinds of variety of this and you can work your way up to head and heels starting with shoulders and lower legs. The idea is to do this and stay there for awhile...you can work up to hours even...the longer the stronger your back. The stronger your back the less likely you are to have back problems. When I was a fat little 12 years old my uncle tried to tell me this could be done simply by crossing your ankles but I never got that to work...this does. Now Iron Shirt takes this exercise farther...once you have gained control of the back muscles you should be able to stretch and literally lift each vertebrae one by one thus releasing nitrous oxide from the joints like when you pop your fingers...I have seen this...still can do it...and that is done just standing.

Now the fastest way to a flat stomach is breathing before you go to sleep at night. You lay flat on your back and breathe in then out as deeply as you can using the yoga count of four for each step to begin with and building it but I suggest you always end it there because its restful and an excellent stress reducer. Breathe in to the count of four...hold it four...out to the count of four...hold that to the count of four. I used to teach my son this trick before a big gymnastics competition and my daughter when she was a kid before a modeling gig...it works on anyone to calm them down. To flatten your belly the trick is to lush to your own extreme the inhale and exhale with your stomach muscles...as far out as you can push your tummy then as far in as you can tighten it...the count is really arbitrary for this but it is how I was taught. Be careful...first time it feels like you can do this forever and it couldn't possibly help...next day you have trouble standing up straight because your tummy muscles hurt so bad... This also aides in digestion.

There is a pressure point between the nose and the upper lip that helps one hold on to consciousness when light headed.

The fastest way to tone body muscle that I have found is to switch back and forth between hot and cold water like shifting from a pool to a hot tub though it can even be obtained though not as well using a shower. The reason this is effective is because it tightens muscles your brain has ignored so long as to not be able to tighten or relax them with cognitive thought. The idea is to stay in one temperature until your core temperature has changed then switch which gets the maximum expansion and contraction and effects the maximum number of muscles.

Remarkably even a few shifts will have some effect. Now it has also been proved that you can alter core temperature by just submerging your hands in water say under a faucet where especially your wrists but the whole hands because of the volume of blood capillaries there changes the actual temperature of the blood flowing through them. This is now being used in cases of hyper and hypothermia. It would then follow that this practice though no doubt more slowly could have the same effect on muscle toning. A cold muscle also cannot heave...discovered it works well to put a cold rag on the stomach of a friend undergoing chemo...

Odds are there is a breathing technique...reason being what is called fire breathing can temporarily increase your body temperature when you are cold. It entails panting like a dog thus bouncing your diaphragm up and down rapidly. The reason I say this is a temporary fix is because it seems to me it disperses core heat which is comforting but in a long term cold situation less than effective over time as your core can cool more quickly however in a situation where your hands are not functional enough to do something you need to do, it can be quite useful!

The original body programming in dire physical circumstance is to protect the core. Then there is the teaching effect of ill health...if you ignore something...some part of your body it will create a circumstance that gets attention. I mention this only because much can be learned if you look from this perspective. For example diabetics have peripheral numbness often followed by skin problems...but rubbing can diminish this cycle of events and if muscle pain isn't felt a skin irritation makes you pay attention to the ignored area so part of what I have learned is to pay attention at first feeling that you should. for example if enduring starvation it may seem counter productive for the pancreas to be first effected but the end result of that cycle would be health effects like diabetes and so forth... It like an advanced program of function and we only know how to play the game...we have much to learn! The Taoists worked at it from this point of view 600 years before Christ. So don't understand the exercises...but they work! These understandings were carried to the point that some claimed to live on air alone...for many years in fact and that is called part of the history of China.

There is one more Taoist exercise but it isn't a specific organ exercise...it's called the Triple Heater. It is said if you do this exercise 28 times in a row you will get rid of a cold almost immediately. I teach it to children to help them get to sleep. It is an excellent relaxation tool. Like the other exercises you use your hands and breathing but this time you lay flat on your back and just hold your arms straight out looking at your palms then you breathe in and raise them over your head only this time as you exhale you make the sound 'heee' lowering your hands with fingers not entwined and palms facing what would be the floor if you were standing from above your head straight down your body like you are pushing something towards your feet then when you reach the length your hands will go you imagine pushing your chi all the way farther to your feet and beyond. I usually get sleepy about the third time but I am conditioned to it...kids tell me it works after about five times for them and they aren't. Now I have to discuss Chi flow. It goes opposite of circulation. it goes up the back and down the front. Gas and as they say heat in the lung is called hot wind rising...its not supposed to go that way. This exercise pushes chi down the front. The brain, the heart, the bowel where the Dan Tien is located are considered heat generators thus the Triple Heater name. That's the simple version. A byproduct of this exercise that I learned that is most useful is the sound alone! It is the sound that prevents straining when pooping! It makes more of you push down than the normal muscles most people use and I know one hemorrhoid damaged friend who swears by it. Enough said...

Unlike western society certain martial arts spend a great deal of time working with muscles we ignore to include the ones that hold all your organs from falling out of you and the cinching ones at your waist that maintain your internal psi. I will merely mention that controlling those muscles can eliminate half of the illnesses caused by poor circulation in those areas and a proficient male martial artist can even control when he will offer his part of fertilization without giving up the prize if you get my drift...lord knows what age will read this! I will not explain that!

To strengthen legs you lie on your back bending your knees so your feet are flat on the floor or bed and then cross one leg over the other (switch them and do this again!). The crossed leg should be where your heel is just past your knee. You pull those toes without hands towards your knee as though you have 'string on a violin between them that you are tightening'...this is how it was described to me and it works. Your ankle becomes stronger and walking easier when you do this regularly. The muscles of the feet atrophy from not walking enough and this exercise strengthens and stretches them.

If you want a strong upper body without going to a gym my first reference would be to buy a tape produced by David Carradine called 'Shaolin Strength Workout' for a full kata but a simplified concept I will include here. Assume a horse riding stance...on each hand hold up your pointer finger folding the other fingers rather naturally and letting the thumb fall naturally which forms the equivalent of 'making a gun' if your hand was at a different angle. You fully extend your arms out to the sides of your body as though pushing walls apart with your palms pointing upwards then you bend at the elbows and bring them to the center of your chest then you push straight out in front of you palms first but still determidly pointing ever upward. You do this with dynamic tensions making your body fight itself in the effort...then you start over. It's that simple and you will have a chest and shoulders like a weight lifter! If you get the tape you will see what a weight lifter _should_ look like! My chiropractor once told me the goal of a healthy back is to be able to hold a pencil between the muscles of the shoulder blades...if you can do that you will never need me again! Surely he jests...

Now the one other thing I would mention here is the 3 Mile Point. This has proved useful to non martial artists I have known. First I have to tell you how to find it. You need to know what a 'chun' is. A 'chun' is a measurement exactly the width of your own finger (or an opponent's but that knowledge isn't needed here). From the knob under your knee cap on your leg you want to look 3 'chun' towards the outside of your body (depending on which leg see?) and 2 'chun' down. You kind of have to apply a great deal of pressure with one finger here. The way to approach a pressure point is to locate it then apply as much pressure as you physically can and it will hurt like hell...that means you actually found the point! Now a point releases in stages...the worst pain will 'give' after a few moments and there is a 'sucking' sensation...I have no better terms to use...sorry...you will feel the pain back off in increments after that until it literally doesn't hurt any more..in fact you can't make it hurt like that again until it needs to be worked again another day. There is a 3 Mile Point on both legs. It is called that because after standing on your feet for a long time or walking a long distance...pressing this point allows you to go 3 more miles...now you know! An excellent skill and great for sore legs at the end of the day too...you can now go farther than the guy who doesn't know this...that's useful!

Sweet kisses are symptomatic of starvation (in the extreme the body digesting the pancreas)...sweet sweat is symptomatic of diabetes. Poopy smelling breathe is symptomatic of liver issues. Urine is absorbed after 7 hours so an ammonia smell to a person may reflect this more than guessing that one has peed themself. These are useful wives tales and not medical diagnosis.

Bleach out plastics...sugar in the bottom of a coffee cup can ferment over night...one needs to consider what makes things grow in a petri dish to think food safety.

For the record I walk with a stick because I think I need to. The dress for my son's wedding isn't tight on me because I am so fat. It's tight on me because my bones are literally deformed...my back x-ray looks a bit like godzilla! Not those little microscopic anomalies doctors normally see and get excited about but great angular spikes of bone. My medical doctor (when I could afford one) started shouting 'Terrible arthritis! Terrible arthritis!' upon seeing my back x-ray. My chiropractor (when I could afford one) took one look at my back x-ray and said, 'Wow! Never saw that before! See the bright edges on the vertebrae? That's the beginnings of osteoporosis but all these spurs are huge! It's like your body is misusing calcium! Wonder what causes that?' Well, that's western medicine for you... In the meantime an empire waistline hits at the base of my sternum which is the only piece of me I have tried to show my daughter to explain not walking so good...it is a gnarled tipped inward knot of bone. The doctors don't understand me...can't afford their help anyway...the family doesn't understand me...and the more I smile and fake it the more they expect. I am not a hunchback but I think my body has that in mind and I argue with it every day. One of the reasons I say I do art because I can do this...there are things I cannot do. It is the martial way to hide an injury or weakness because it gives an opponent knowledge of where you can be hurt. I don't complain...it's self defeating. My experience is I scare my children with words when they hear what's wrong with me and I just shock doctors. It doesn't matter. This is my body and my life and how I handle it is simply choice and options...let's hope I don't make a serious mistake and have all the right options! (Plinko! Humanity!) I'm trying not to make mistakes every day...

I watched my husband with his bad back carry water from the tub upstairs in a five gallon bucket to flush the downstairs toilet and told him I was sorry I couldn't do it myself yesterday...he declared himself the KIng of Poop and plodded on. This morning I watched him do the same thing again and wanted to cry because I know it hurts his back but said nothing. Been writing all night and about to lay down now...gee...gotta go...walk into the bathroom half asleep and debate the light switch then flip it on...use tissue to open the pot because you always leave it closed when you only flush once a day and tissue because you never feel like you can get your hands clean washing them from a jug of water even though you probably do...I went then without a second thought stood like a normal person and flushed the toilet! No! I said out loud! No...

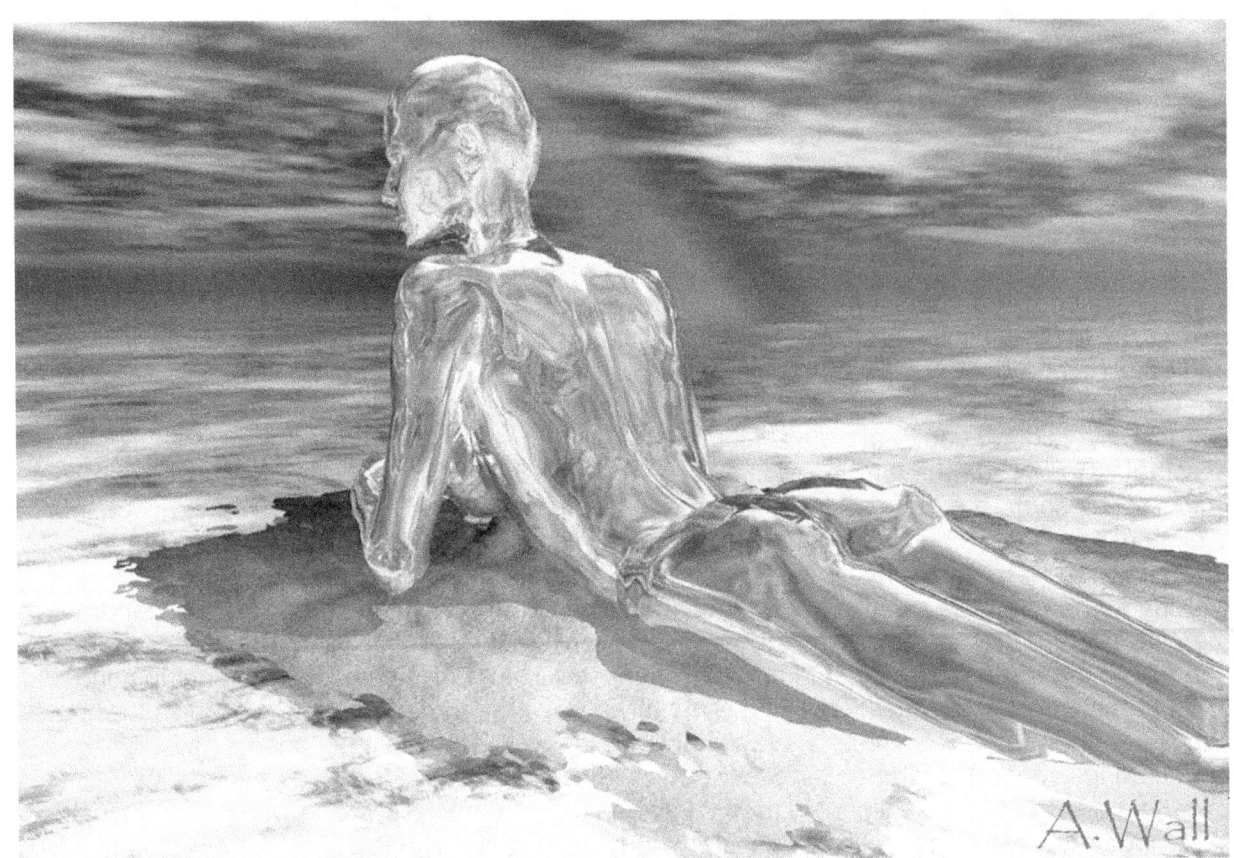

CHAPTER SEVEN

Its been raining heavily for several days now afterall this is Florida and hurricane season. It's a funny feeling when its pouring outside and your water is turned off. Water, water everywhere and...well you know...

You know having written all these things you might think I am a person feeling sorry for myself but that only comes in small increments over time and I refuse to allow it to drive my life. Instead thoughts come to mind like the song of the Little Drummer Boy. And people wonder why I'm such an optimist...that's a survival skill too. I hope here I have given you enough to be curious about to give you course for thought...both also survival skills...curiosity and thoughtfulness. I also hope you like the art I have thrown in that I believe in...that is my real hope incarnate. Beauty warms the soul...

In closing, I want to go back to my art. I had almost given up and quit just sitting and wondering what would come of me. It began at Christmas when I had no gifts and no one had time to come see me. I began producing a computerized Christmas Gift of Family Recipes and quotes I could possibly mail to all my kids and I just lost heart somewhere in the middle...I never finished the project...there just were no gifts from me for the first time in my life. There were no gifts for any of my children's birthdays...very little for my daughter's wedding but a lot of effort to try to make money myself because my husband still had no luck but my art got ignored beyond that for a time, I sat a lot from Christmas until early summer barely working my garden even. It isn't depression when you just don't know what to do anymore...I had no feelings of worthlessness or other things they tell you to look for...just created the habit of sitting instead of doing...my husband and I worked on better communications...we talked more...I quit blaming us so much and began to just wonder what would happen next

Then came my granddaughter's fifth birthday...last one before she embarks on the public school system and becomes what the world will make of her. I couldn't go to her party...couldn't get there from here even though I had put the bug in my daughter's ear that my son was short and she should throw it so she did. I had no gift to send. Somewhere in the middle of the party my daughter decided to call me to let me know the party occurred and it was just too hard to get me there and besides there was no time to do it...then there's always the mention of gas money which I don't have to offer. She put my granddaughter on the phone so I could say the words. I put on my happiest voice and wished her a happy birthday but almost got tearful trying to explain that if I could I would not only be there but would buy her lots of presents...she's a remarkable child...she caught the slip in my voice. She calmly said to me...'I know what you want grandmommy', and proceeded to tell me a story intended to cheer me up! She said I would make a bunch of presents and put them all in a drawer and close the drawer making sure it wasn't too high so she could reach it and then she would open the drawer and find all the presents and say look what my granmommy made for me! I told her she was right and made her swear she was having fun then got off the phone and cried like a baby. How immensely profound the voice of that small child! She was right! She was right... I considered my situation...my predicament... I considered the time all of this was flatly stealing from me... I considered what a life is and what it should mean to those you leave behind... I considered the helplessness and uncertainty of my life... I considered what I would leave should this mess kill me tomorrow cause I never thought myself smart enough to have all the answers and more often than not lives end because someone make a mistake...that could happen to me whether I argue with death to the best of my ability every day or not and I do! What would I leave? After my daughter's wedding it was said that I hadn't been involved enough by the daughter-in-law to be in ten days and I had even less to offer her wedding in the form of things...but I have my art! That's where my Zazzle obsession began...I can show intent...I can store it in cyber space to outlast robberies...utilities...or even me! I could have my lifetime back...I could express my feelings...I could show my will by producing art in cyber space! So I do...

One day my best effort will likely be defragged out of a mainframe somewhere...how Johnny Mneumonic of me!

I am reminded of a song from my childhood by Elton John...I used to like it! Still do...

If I were a Carpenter but then again no...or a man who made potions in a travelling show...I know it ain't much but it's the best I can do...my gift is my song and...this one's for you...

The damages of a life well lived consume me...old age possesses me and there is no grace.

I am a Starving Artist...and this is my song...

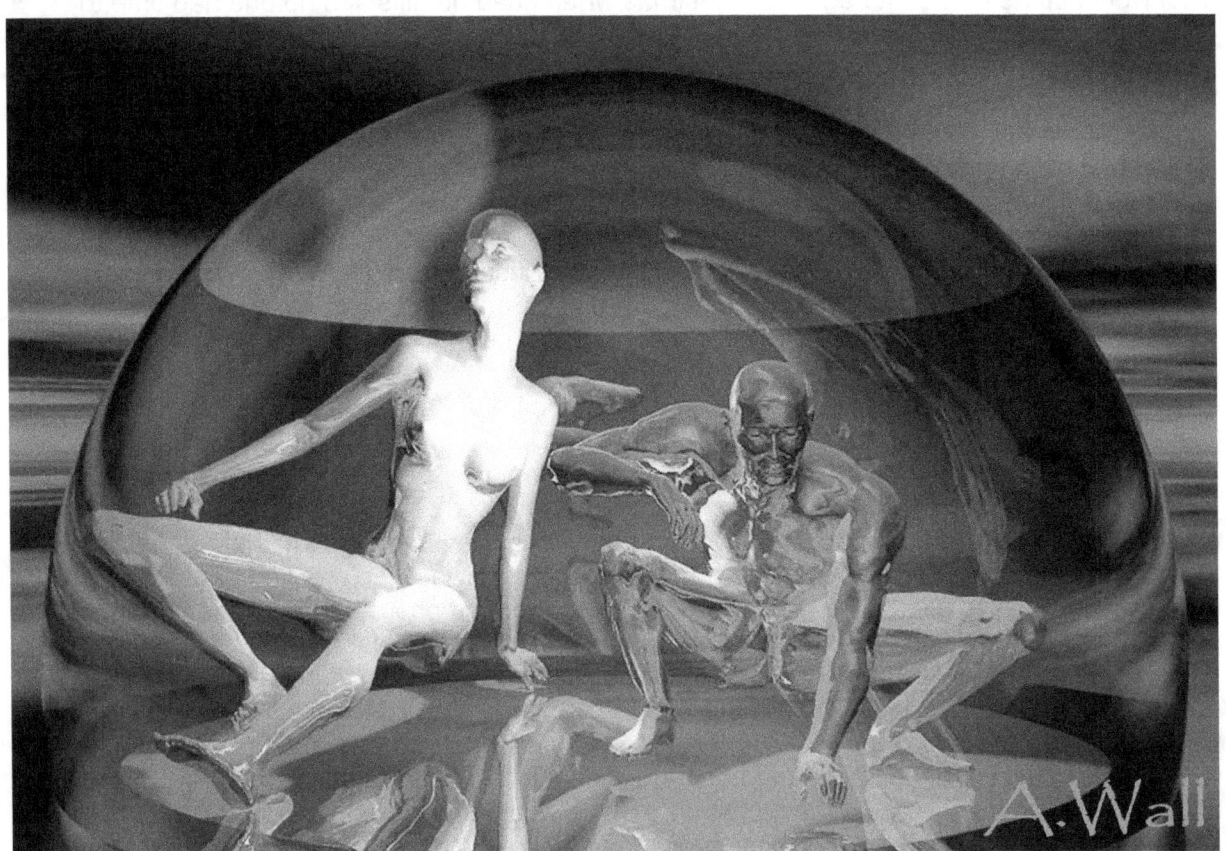

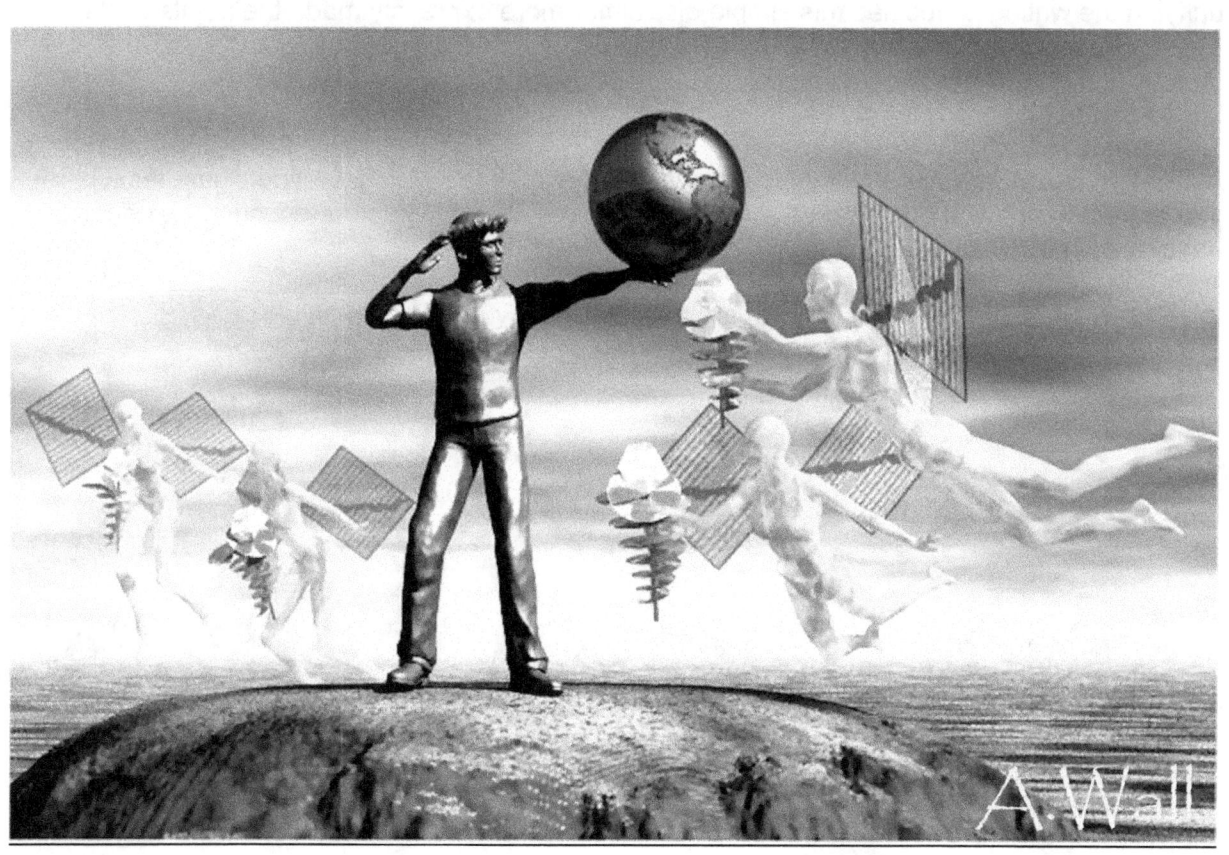

AFTERTHOUGHT~ Please take into considerations that what appears to be inconsistencies and changes in writing style in this offering are caused by changed states of being of the author and writing style. I chose to come back and add things to pieces already written as they came to mind. My physical state fluctuates with financial situation and my state of mind changes as well. My writing style is to write until my back hurts badly enough that I have to move. I got more sleep after my water went off and better food after our stamps came in...I began writing this time after throwing out all our refrigerated goods when my lights went off because I got food poisoning from a bbq sauce we thought had survived the ordeal just before attempting this writing. I found that as I wrote and things changed I would recall something over looked or find the clarity to write a broader opinion. Looking at the effort after the fact with the intention of unifying the writing...I decided this simple disclaimer more expressly made the points written here.

I hope this book does what my daughter thinks it will and save me from this cycle of events...

ANSWER: Because you have to give away cigarettes to those who gave you cigarettes when you had none and you don't want them touching all the filters...who knows where their hands have been??? (I was taught that...)

Wall sized prints of this art (and more) are available at www.zazzle.com/Neophyle

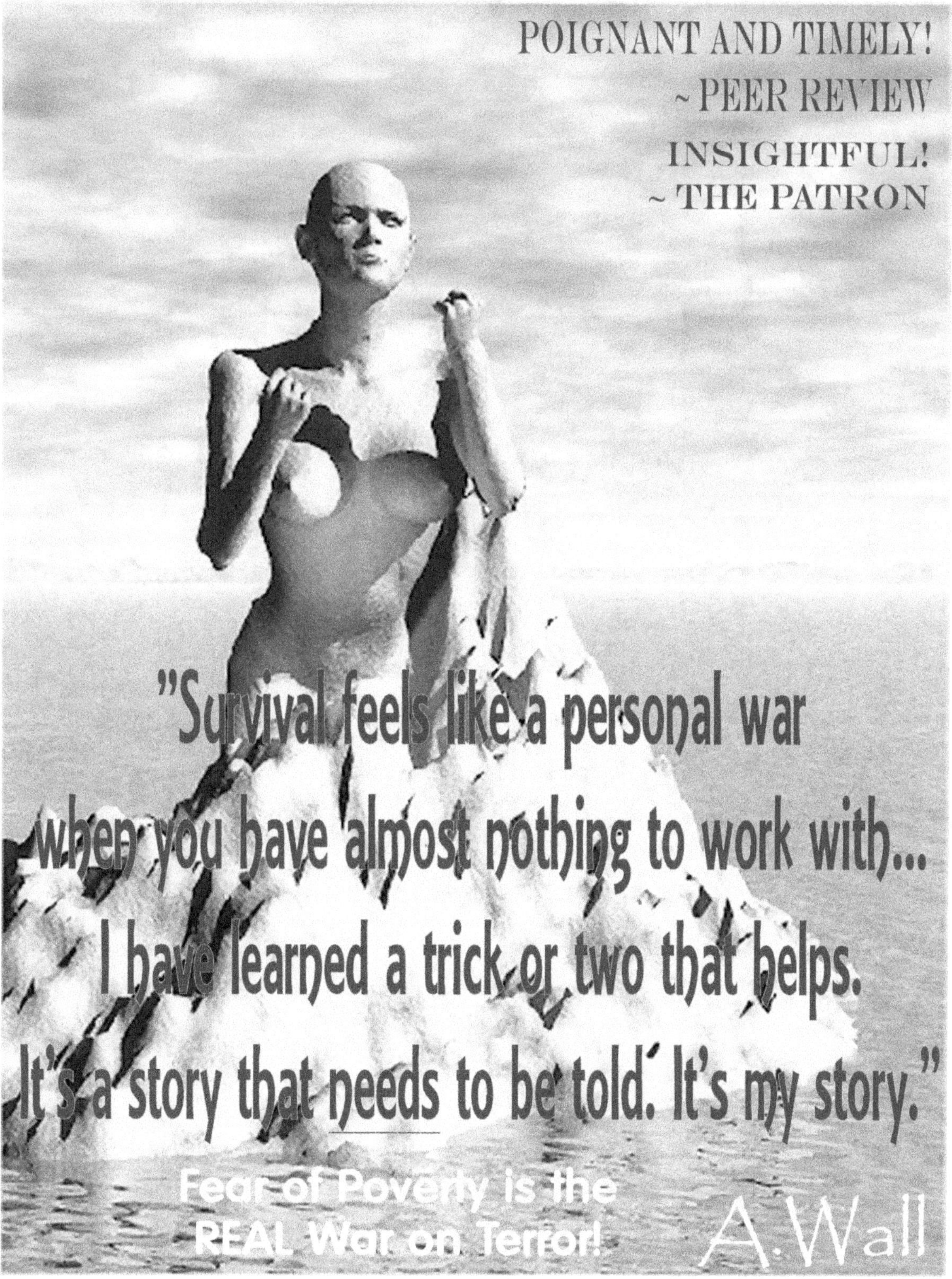
POIGNANT AND TIMELY!
~ PEER REVIEW
INSIGHTFUL!
~ THE PATRON
"Survival feels like a personal war
when you have almost nothing to work with...
I have learned a trick or two that helps.
It's a story that needs to be told. It's my story."
Fear of Poverty is the
REAL War on Terror!
A.Wall